100 Easy-To...

10.

Dear,
MRS. S. ROTHERHAM.
MR. B. ROTHERHAM.

Thanks for being with
us. All the best.
"We will miss you".
Padma
HOTEL MIRA
CALANGUTE.
GOA.
Ph. 0832-276023

100 Easy-To-Make
Punjabi Dishes

Bimal M Singh

TARANG PAPERBACKS
a division of
VIKAS PUBLISHING HOUSE PVT LTD

VIKAS PUBLISHING HOUSE PVT LTD
576, Masjid Road, Jangpura, New Delhi-110 014

Reprint 1993

Printed at Sanjay Printers, Delhi-110 032.

To
my mother Parkash Kaur
with
love and admiration

Introduction

Punjabi cooking and eating is just like the Punjabis themselves ; it is simple and forthright, sizable and hearty. Again, like a Punjabi whose life is highly priortized, Punjabi cooking is neither stylized nor for that matter choreographed, to borrow a phrase from the world of arts.

Punjabi cooking has no unnecessary frills or embellishments. If that be a deficiency, it is more than made up by a Punjabi's utterly inimitable, verbal imagery of *"Aao Ji, Baitho Ji, Khao Ji"*. That is to say, "Welcome, sit down and eat". Of course, no prior introductions are necessary. These waste time and can be taken care of after eating is over ! Or wait till you meet your Punjabi hosts next time ! A Punjabi, as an incorrigible optimist believes most ardently that there would always be a next time to meeting you and more than that to treating you to yet another manifestation of Punjabi's gusty, lusty images of hospitality.

Punjabi folklore expresses so exquisitely the kind of elemental and intense life that the Punjabis live. A popular adage celebrates the virtues of "eating well and ploughing hard". It is in the nature of a rage to live. Someone, who was not an anatomist, said that a Punjabi's heart is bigger than his stomach. It is this passion for bigness which gives his pursuits an acquisitive dimension of monster-like trucks and still larger tractors. It sets him out to seek his destiny and fulfilment across infinite spaces and the seven seas in quest of huge farms. Each time you share a Punjabi meal, there is something of a warmth about its being hot that wafts itself in a peculiar flavour. It arches the metallic "thalis" like a rainbow of culinary colours.

My predominant emotion in writing this book was to evoke these very joys of eating. A time it was when "Daal" and "Saag" simmered slowly in earthen ovens, carved out of the walls, with pristine images of birds and animals etched in mud. With Punjabis now jet-set against time, with pressures and tensions boiling now in pressure cookers, a joy has gone out of our lives.

But it can come back too if it is retrieved out of the bylanes of memories. In doing this book, I relied on my own memories and the rich repertory of recipes which old ladies rolled out of their white-haired memories with nostalgia and at times with tears. Sitting in their company and chatting with them, the picture of a large sprawling Punjab came back alive with a sense of urgency. When from these "remembrances of things past" I came back with a jerk to the contemporary situation, I realised how things had shrunk with Punjab's five rivers amputated to two and a half dried up memories of dammed monsoon furies.

But it was heartening too, that so much of the genuine Punjabi cooking still survived in homes and in Dhabas, in far away villages and in the narrow winding alleys of cities like Amritsar. Amritsar was and in many ways still is, the culinary capital of Punjab. This sadly enough does not make much of a news. But that is where you can still eat seven layered "tandoori prarthas" in all their crisp and greasy glory. You have part of this Punjabi cooking still surviving in the little Punjabs that are dotted all over the world map and stretch from Southall to California.

My book is for all those who would like to share the joys of Punjabi eating and for those Punjabis especially who are rootlessly adrift on the waves of time. My string of recipes is also for all those people who would again share meals with each other and build up new bridges of love and understanding. In writing this, I have experienced strong emotions of joy and sorrow and of nostalgia and hope I have put my memories into "katories" and laid them on "thalis".

New Delhi   Bimal M. Singh
March 1987

A Time to Write : A Time to Thank

I cannot acknowledge in words my very sincere gratitude for all those who have helped me in putting these images of Punjabi cooking together.

My mother, Smt Parkash Kaur and mother-in-law, Smt Gurbachan Kaur, helped me in not only suggesting recipes out of their memories but also in working them out patiently. It has been an unforgettable experience learning from them.

My special thanks are due to Shiela Bhatia, Bimla Khosla, Maninder and Tarlochan Sandhu, Mrs I.P. Singh, R. Kasthia of Claridges Hotel and Manu Mehta of Maurya Sheraton. They suggested and shared memories of recipes and images of contemporary variations on a theme of Punjabi cooking.

I am indebted to my brother Percy for his invaluable suggestions in bringing out this book in its final shape.

And how can I ever forget Prem, our cook, who willingly, patiently experimented and worked out the recipes with me. His was the toil and mine was the joy.

I am indebted too to all those who appreciated food on my table. They are nameless and yet not forgotten and they shall always be welcome and make life worth living and more than that worth cooking for.

And how can I ever forget my husband, Man Mohan Singh and my two children, Vikram and Gautam, for whom I have cooked all these years and whose joy in eating has given me a kind of happiness that words can never express. Man Mohan's love for Punjabi food always encouraged me to strive for and yet not achieve that elusive point of perfection. That search has been a part of my cooking odyssey.

Handy Do's and Don'ts

1. To get best taste and flavour of food serve freshly cooked food. Frozen and reheated food loses its taste. Fresh salad always complements the food. Whole onions peeled and squashed, green chillies, fresh and tender and ginger go well with Punjabi food. Pickles and Chutneys made from seasonal vegetables add to the taste.

2. Cooking done in Degkchi and Karahi on slow fire tastes better.

3. Pure ghee and fresh butter made from fresh cream enhance the taste and flavour of the food.

4. For rotis wheat flour dough kneaded in advances makes better rotis. For Makki-di-Roti, knead the flour with hot water and make rotis immediately.

5. Fresh coriander is handy to garnish the dishes. A small patch grown in a garden is very useful.

6. Wheat flour or maize flour should be stored carefully. With prolonged and faulty storage, it goes stale and tastes foul.

7. For Pilau use long grained rice called 'Basmati'. Quality of rice improves with storage.

8. Vegetables should be washed before they are peeled and sliced.

9. Leafy vegetables like spinach fenugreek and mustard-greens should be washed in ample water to remove grains of sand and soil.

10. Any vegetable refined oil can be used if pure ghee cooking is not preferred for slimming reasons !

11. Mixed dry spices can be powdered and kept. If kept for too long the flavour is lost.

12. For gravy masala, onion ginger garlic can be liquidized, or grated and ground.

13. Dried fenugreek and mint leaves can be stored and used for flavouring.

14. Milk boiled and cooled gives excellent fresh cream (Malai). Top layer of the milk is used as cream mixed into a paste with little milk.

15. Curds set in earthen pot (kunda) sets and tastes better.

Handy measures :

All measures used in the book are level measures unless stated otherwise.

Use tea cup for a cup 2 tsps for dessertspoon and, 3 tsps for 1 tbsp.

Notes :   tsp reads teaspoon.
               tbsp reads tablespoon.

Cooking Medium

Punjabi food cooked in pure ghee tastes delicious. In many homes pure ghee is still used for cooking. Since pure ghee food is heavy to digest and creates cholesterol problems, refined ground nut oil is preferred. Most of the recipes given are cooked in refined groundnut oil. Pure ghee and fresh butter used in certain recipes enhance the taste and flavour. Dishes like halwa, saag, daal, without pure ghee will not have the real taste and flavour. For deep frying, vanaspati ghee is preferred. Sarson oil (mustard oil) is preferred for making pakoras.

Contents

Beverages

Cold drinks are a boon in hot summer. Flavoured lassi and Badam sharbat in summer are cooling and refreshing.

"*Gajar kanji*" is appetising before lunch in winter. And Seera substitutes the soup in winter as a filling, nourishing and medicinal joy. (*Helps bad cold and heavy head.*)

1. Sattoo
2. Chatti-wali-lassi
3. Badam sharbat
4. Shardai
5. Gajar kanji
6. Amb ras
7. Seera
8. Dodhi

1

Sattoo (Barley-Powder-Drink)

Barley—roasted and ground coarsely—2 tbsp
Jaggery (Shakkar)—2 tbsp
Water—250 ml

Roast barley and grind it while it is still warm. Make syrup with jaggery and water, add barley powder, stir and drink before it starts thickening.

It is an excellent summer drink.

2

Chatti-wali-Lassi

Traditional lassi (Butter milk) is made from well—set curds made from cow's or buffalo's milk. It is churned well till butter separates and floats on top and enough water is added. Butter milk from which butter is separated is nourishing, very cooling in summer and is good for health. It is taken with salt and pepper or sugar.

> *Salted Butter Milk (1 large glass)*
> *Curd—250 gms (well set)*
> *Water—100 ml*
> *Salt and pepper to taste*
> *Ground cumin seeds—½ tsp*

Beat or churn curd—add water, salt and pepper.

Add cumin powder, and crushed ice to serve garnished with mint leaves.

Use wooden churner (madhani) to churn the curd.

Matha (Sweetened butter milk) : add two tbsp., sugar to churned curd instead of salt and pepper. It tastes far better with jaggery instead of sugar.

3

Badam Sharbat (Almond Sharbat)

A cooling and nourishing summer drink.

Almonds—50 (100 gms)
Green cardamoms—15-20

Grind together almonds and cardamoms with skin and with little water. Then strain through muslin cloth. Again grind with some water and squeeze, to repeat it till the juice is extracted to the last drop. It is easier if done in the electric liquidiser.

Syrup: for 1/2 litre juice—*750 gms sugar.*

In 250 ml water dissolve sugar and make syrup. Add 5 gms of citric acid. Cool the syrup. Add almond juice. Add 1 gm sodium benzoate for preservation. If almond sharbat is to be consumed in two-three days, one can keep the bottle in refrigerator and avoid putting the preservative.

This sharbat added to milk and shaken up with crushed ice in the liquidiser makes an excellent flavoured milk. Or dilute sharbat with three parts with cold water and ice.

4

Shardai (A Summer Cooler)

Almonds (Soaked and peeled)—15
Poppy Seeds—1 tbsp
Magaz—1 tsp
Peppercorns—5
Milk—250 ml
Sugar—4 tbsp. or to taste
Water—1/2 cup to grind the ingredients
Water—250 ml

Soak poppy seeds, magaz and cardamoms for 30 minutes. Grind almonds, poppy seeds, magaz, and sugar. Grind well by sprinkling water, add half cup water, strain and squeeze well though muslin cloth, and then add remaining water and milk. Chill it for a cold drink.

An ideal drink in dry heat it makes a refreshing and nourishing cold drink and is favourite with Punjabis.

5

Gajar Kanji (Carrot Juice)

A tangy winter appetizer—Red Wine of Punjab.

Fresh black carrots—1/2 kg
Salt—4 tbsps.
Red chillies powder—1½ tsp
Mustard powder (Rye)—2 tsp
Water—3½ litres (15 cups)
Ceramic or earthen jar (matka)

Wash and scrape carrots. Cut each carrot lengthwise into 3-4 pieces. Mix mustard powder, salt and chillies with water, add carrots, pour into earthen or ceramic jar and cover the mouth with muslin cloth. Keep the jar in the sun for 2-3 days and stir it everyday. The colour of kanji will be red-purple. It can be kept in the refrigerator and used as required. Small pieces of carrot can be served along with it.

Note: Use ordinary carrots and add beet-root for colour, if black carrots are not available.

7

6

Amb Ras (Raw Mango Pulp Juice)

Raw mangoes—1/2 kg
Sugar— 400 gms
Water
Dry masala powder :

Masala : *Tymol seeds—3tsp.* Roast on girddle (Tawa) and powder together
Cuminseed — 4 tsp.
Black salt—1tsp.
Salt—3tsp.
Mix altogether

Peel and cut mangoes. Cook in enough water to cover the fruit. Mash the pulp, add sugar and cook for a few minutes. Then sieve the pulp.

Roast and powder tymol seeds and cuminseed. Add white and black salt.

Put 2 tbsp. pulp in a glass, add ½ tsp. masala powder, cold water and stir. Serve it cold.

It is cooling and refreshing in summer.

Masala: *Tymol seeds—3 tsp.* Roast on griddle (Tawa)
Cuminseed—4 tsp. Powder altogether.
Black salt—1 tsp.
Salt—3 tsp.

7

Seera

(Fried gram flour in sugar syrup)—makes 1 cup (hot drink).

Gram flour (vesan)—1/2 tbsp.
Water—1¼ cup
Sugar—2 tsp.
Pure ghee—2 tsp.
One brown cardamom seeds (moti elaichi)
Chopped almonds—4

Heat ghee—add Semolina or gram flour, Cardamom and fry on slow fire . Make syrup with sugar and water—add to the roasted gram flour or semolina and boil—till it thickens a bit. Serve it hot garnished with chopped almonds.

For Semolina: *Semolina—2 tsp.*

Water—2 cups
Sugar—3 tsp.

8

Dodhi

Milk flavoured and enriched with cardamom and almonds

Poppy seeds—2 tbsp. level
Magaz—1 tbsp. level
Green cardamom—6
Almonds—20 soaked in ½ cup water
Sugar to taste—3 tbsp
Pure ghee—1 tbsp
Milk—½ litre
Water—½ cup

Soak poppy seeds—magaz and cardamom in half a cup of water overnight. Grind it to a fine paste—adding little water. Add sugar and grind, add water and sieve. Grind almonds separately. Add to the prepared liquid. Heat pure ghee and add the prepared liquid to it.

On slow fire—keep it stirring, fry till it is light golden, dry the liquid and add milk. Keep stirring till it is thick and only two cups of liquid remain. Serve it hot.

Milk-based Preparations

Milk is synonymous with the land of Punjab Milk is a vital part of Punjabi diet. Flavoured milk is now a popular drink.

Various milk products add to variety in food and are a part of daily diet, like Dahi, Lassi, Panir, Butter, Ghee, Cream and various other products.

Punjabi food is just incomplete without milk preparations.

Butter :

Butter is an important part of a Punjabi meal. A typical and much relished Punjabi breakfast consists of plain roti, butter and lassi. Freshly made butter is used to grease rotis, plain or tandoori. Butter is added to daals, saag, etc. before serving a dish. Butter cooking has its own flavour and brings out the subtle tastes of each dish. It is a delicious cooking medium. Butter collected over a few days is heated and turned into (Desi) pure ghee—so vital to Punjabi cooking, diet and thinking.

Pure Desi Ghee (Clarified Butter) :

Pure ghee made from cream or butter is a vital cooking medium in many Punjabi homes, especially in the villages. Despite the cholestrol problem still many Punjabi families cannot dispense with Pure Ghee as a cooking medium or as an addition to the cooked food, like daal and saag etc. Various sweets are prepared with desi ghee like gajrela halwa, (gram flour) vesan-di-barfi, pinnies etc. Ghee and shakkar go very well with makki-di-roti. Just cannot be resisted !

Dahi (Curds)

Curds can be set by adding curd culture to warm milk and is allowed to set for a few hours. The proportion of culture and duration of time taken for setting varies with season. Curds set in kundas (Earthen pot) sets and tastes better. Curds are used in cooking also. They add to the flavour and taste of the dish. They are used as marinating and thickening agents.

9. Punjabi Karhi
10. Dall Ladoo
11. Dahi Bhalle
12. Khoya Bhaaji
13. Panir Kofta
14. Matter Panir
15. Methi Panir
16. Malai Panir

Punjabi Karhi (Butter Milk—Curry)

Sour curd —1 kg
Gram flour—1 cup
Water—1 litre
Onions—2 chopped
Garlic—6 cloves
Ginger—1" piece
Salt—2 tsp.
Cooking oil—3 tbsp

Spices
Mustard (Rye) —1 tsp
Fenugreek (Methi)—½ tsp
Nigella (Kalauji)—1½ tsp
Coriander seeds (Dhania)—1 tsp
Cuminseed (Jeera)—½ tsp

Roast these on tawa and grind them to powder. Chopped coriander—50 grams.

Pakoras (Dumplings). Gram flour—250 grams, Sliced onions, potatoes, green chillies fenugreek or spinach chopped, salt—1 tsp., mixed spices—1 tsp., and mustard oil to fry.

Grind garlic, ginger to a paste. Heat oil in a pan. Fry the paste brown, add chopped onions and fry them light brown. Keep aside. Make batter with gram flour, add water, salt and mixed spices. Beat well till it is light and fluffy. Add onion, potato slices and chillies or chopped fenugreek. Heat oil in a Karahi, and smoke the oil. Make pakoras with vegetables dipped in the batter.

Beat curds, add gram flour and water and stir well. Add this to the fried onion-ginger garlic paste. Add salt and powdered masalas to it. Bring it to boil, lower the heat. Cook for 10-15 minutes (stirring frequently) till it coats the back of the ladle (Karchi), add pakoras and chopped coriander. Cover and keep it aside. Heat before serving.

Karhi goes well with boiled rice.

Note: Mixed vegetables like carrots, cauliflower, potatoes, onions, chillies etc. can be added to Karhi instead of Pakoras.

Curd Variations

Raita variations: Curd is beaten with salt-pepper chillies added to it. In addition these variations can be made:

1. *Cucumber*: Peeled and grated, water squeezed and added to the beaten curd.
2. *Ghia*: Scraped, grated and boiled-water squeezed and added to the curd.
3. *Round brinjal*: Smoked on open fire, peeled, washed and mashed to be added to curd.
4. *Kichnar buds*: Boiled squeezed and added to the curd.
5. *Potatoes*: Boiled and cut into pieces added to the curd.
6. *Pakori*: Gram flour batter deep fried as small balls (through the sieve it is squeezed into hot oil).
7. *Dahi bhalla*: Made with soaked and ground pulse.
8. *Moong daal ladoos*:

To the raita add finely chopped onions, ginger, green chillies and coriander leaves. Garnish with red chilli powder pepper and mint leaves.

10

Daal Ladoo

Dhoti Moong daal—100 gms
Water to soak daal
Salt—½ tsp.
Cuminseed—½ tsp
Oil for frying
Soda bi-carb—$\frac{1}{8}$ tsp
Curds—½ kg

Wash daal. Soak in enough water to cover the daal. Soak for two hours. Drain the water and grind it to fine paste. Add salt, cuminseed and soda. Mix it well. Keep it aside for ten minutes. Heat oil in a frying pan or karahi. Put the paste in forms of small balls into hot ghee and fry them light golden.

Soak them in cold water and cover. Press water out of each ball. (1/2 kg).

Put balls in the dish and pour beaten curd over it. Garnish with coriander leaves and chaat masala.

Imli chutney goes well with it. The thought of it makes your mouth water!

11

Dahi Bhalle

Urad washed—250 gm
Water to soak daal
Onion—1 chopped finely
Ginger—small pieces—chopped
Green coriander—chopped
Green chillies—2 chopped
Cuminseed—$\frac{1}{2}$ tsp
Salt—$\frac{1}{2}$ tsp
Soda-bi—carb—$\frac{1}{4}$ tsp
Oil for frying
Curds—750 gm
Raisins—15-20

Wash and soak daal in enough water to cover the daal. Soak it for 3 hrs. Drain water and grind, add chopped onion, ginger, coriander-chillies-salt cuminseed and soda. Heat oil. With moistened hands, make Bhalla with daal batter into 2" discs.

Deep fry—each Bhalla—light brown. Drain oil, keep aside. Soak in hot water for ten minutes. Press out water lightly. Beat curds—add salt—$\frac{1}{2}$ tsp. cuminseed. Soak—raisins in water for ten minutes. Add to the curd.

Lay Bhallas in a flat dish—pour curds on it, garnish with red chilli powder-chopped coriander, powdered cumin-seed.

Serve with Imli chutney and extra beaten curd.

Khoya (Dried Fresh Milk)

It is another milk product, used mainly for making sweets. It is prepared from milk by cooking (buffalo's milk has more fat content) to the consistency of thick porridge. Milk has to be stirred constantly while it is cooking. It enriches the dish it is added to. Different kinds of mithais are made from khoya. Delicious rabri is made with khoya cooked in milk.

12

Khoya Bhaaji

Curds—150 gms
Khoya—100 gms
Makhana—25 gms
Cooking oil—4 tbsp
Cloves garlic—6
Ginger—1" piece] grind together
Tomatoes—2
Onion—1 large
Shelled peas—boiled—1/2 cup
Salt to taste
Garam masala—1/2 tsp
Turmeric powder—1 tsp
Red chilli powder—1/2 tsp
Chopped coriander leaves to garnish

Heat 1 tbsp. cooking oil, add khoya, fry it on slow fire till it is light brown in colour. Put 1 tbsp. cooking oil in a separate pan—add curds and fry for sometime. Fry masala with grated onion, add ginger garlic paste. Add chopped tomatoes and fry. Add curds then khoya and stir nicely. Add cooked peas. Fry makhanas lightly and add. Add little water to simmer for a few minutes and let the water dry. Serve it garnished with chopped coriander leaves.

It is a rich vegetarian dish, looks and tastes close to mince meat (keema) dish.

Panir (Cottage Cheese) :

Panir is made from curdled milk and after draining—it is set and cut into pieces or used unset. It is rich in nutrition and is wholesome. Panir with salt and pepper tastes even setter.

1. Panir-koftas
2. Matar-panir
3. Methi-panir
4. Malai-panir

Panir-Making (Cottage Cheese)

Panir is made by curdling the milk. Curd lemon juice or vinegar can be used to curdle the milk.

Boil the milk—add 1/2 cup curd to 1 litre milk or juice of one lemon or 1 tbsp. vinegar. Milk will separate, immediately, if not, add more of curding agent panir and the liquid will separate. Remove from fire, drain the liquid (whey). Whey is tasty and full of nourishment and can be used to make gravy.

Set the panir by putting it in thin cloth and pressing it under weight for about half an hour.

13

Panir Kofta
(Cottage Cheese Balls in Gravy.)

Panir --200 gms from 1 litre whole milk
Filling:
Ghee—1 tsp.
Panir—1 tbsp.
Finely cut green chillies—1
Red chillies ¼ tsp.
Fresh coriander leaves—1 tbsp.
Pista shredded—10 pieces
Salt—¼ tsp.
Raisins—16
Flour—1½ tbsp.
Onion grated—1 tbsp.
Gravy :
Ginger—1" piece
Garlic—6 cloves
Onions grated—3
Cooking oil—4 tbsp.
Almonds chopped—6
Green chillies chopped—2
Sugar—1/2 tsp.
Salt—1½ tsp
Tomatoes chopped—100gms

Garam masala—$\frac{1}{2}$ *tsp*
Degi Mirach—1/4 tsp. (for colour)
Poppy seeds (Khas Khas)—1 tsp.
Soak poppy seeds and grind to a paste, chopped coriander leaves
Water—1 cup
Ghee or oil for frying

Make panir drain off the liquid and keep it for the gravy.

Heat the ghee and fry lightly finely grated onions. Add 25 gms crumbled panir, salt, red pepper raisin, pista finely cut ginger, green chillies coriander leaves and stir. Remove from fire and leave it to cool. Divide it into 10 parts.

Balls: Knead the remaining panir with the palm of hand till the grains disappear. Add flour or an egg to bind the panir mixture. Add salt, red chillies, garam masala. Knead a little. Divide it into 10 parts and flatten. Put a part of the filling on each and with the help of the (panir water) whey shape into round balls. Fry in ghee on a medium heat till it is golden brown. Remove from the ghee—drain and leave them till required.

Gravy: Heat the ghee and fry the onions lightly. Add chillies, ground ginger, garlic, almonds cuminseed, poppy seeds, chopped tomatoes, sugar and salt. Continue frying, add a table spoon full of whey and water and simmer on slow fire till it is reduced to two-third. Add the panir balls just before serving and heat thoroughly. Sprinkle coriander leaves-green chillies. Serve it immediately,

14

Mattar-Panir (Peas and Cottage Cheese)

Shelled-Peas—2 cups
Cottage cheese—250 gms
Onion—2
Ginger—1" piece
Garlic—4-6 cloves
Tomatoes— 2
Coriander leaves—a small bunch
Salt—1 tsp
Red chilli powder--1/2 tsp
Oil—2 tbsp

Cut the cottage cheese in pieces and lightly fry and keep aside. Grind coriander leaves fine, add little water. Chop onions, ginger and garlic and crush them. Heat oil in a pan and fry the paste well, add tomatoes, salt, turmeric powder and chilli powder, fry till the oil separates from the masala. Add peas and fry a little—add coriander paste. Add enough water, cook the peas. Add fried cottage cheese pieces. Simmer for a few minutes.

Methi Panir (Cottage Cheese and Fenugreek)

Make Panir from 1 litre milk cut into squares and lightly fry them.

Fenugreek (fresh)—750 gms, chop, wash and sprinkle salt on the leaves, let it stand for 10 minutes, squeeze out the bitter juice.

Beaten curds—2 tbsp
Cooking oil —4 tbsp
Chopped onion—1
Chopped tomato—1
Ginger chopped—½" piece
Salt to taste
Chillies and coriander powders.

Heat oil—add onions and ginger to it—fry a bit, add methi, cover it and let it cook. Add salt, chillies, let it cook. Add curds and chopped tomato. Let it cook. Add the fried panir and mix and let it cook for a while on slow fire. (Clean spinach and chop the spinach—wash well. Spinach can be used instead of methi—no salt to be rubbed on spinach.) Pressure cook spinach—grind it well then add to the fried onion and ginger, cook, add curd and chopped tomato.

Malai Panir (Cottage Cheese in Cream)

Cottage Cheese—250 gms
Chopped onion—1
garlic—3 to 4 cloves pounded
Pureed tomato—1
Ginger sliced—1" piece
Dried Fenugreek
leaves—2 tsp
Cooking oil—2 tbsp
Cream—¾ cup
Salt to taste
Green chillies—chopped in long pieces.

Slice cottage cheese into pieces. Heat oil-fry garlic, add onions and ginger, add tomatoes and fry for three-four minutes. Add chopped chillies and then sliced cottage cheese and fenugreek leaves cover and gently cook for 2-3 minutes, add cream, lower the heat and toss gently. Serve it hot.

Snacks

17. Panir pakora
18. Amritsari tali machhi
19. Alu tikki
20. Mixed vagetables tikki

Panir Pakora (Cottage Cheese Pakora)

Panir-cut into long strips 2" long ½" wide.
Batter
Gram flour (Vesan)—120 gms
Clove garlic—4
Ginger—½" piece
Green chilli chopped—1
Salt—1 tsp
Chilli powder—¼ tsp
Coriander powder—2 tsp
Chaat Masala—1 tsp
Mixed Spices—1 tsp
Mustard oil or cooking oil for frying
Water to make batter of medium consistency.
Soda bi—carb—¼ tsp

Sift the gram flour in a basin. Make a well in the centre. Gradually add water, stirring, beat well-add the rest of the water, soda and put it away for sometime. Add salt, chilli powder, ground paste of ginger and clove-coriander powder —beat well. Dip panir strips and fry in hot oil. Sprinkle chaat masala and serve it hot with mint chutney.

Vegetable Pakoras

In the same batter add sliced onions. Cauliflower Spinach leaves green chillies or sliced potatoes can be dipped and fried.

Cut vegetables, put salt and chillies and put aside. Put in a plate for extra water to drain off. Dip in the batter and deep fry.

Serve with mint chutney.

Amritsari Tali Machhi (Fried Fish)

Fish—3/4 kg.
Juice of lemon—1½ lemon
Salt—1½ tsps
Chilli-powder—1½ tsp
Mango powder (Amchoor)—½tsp
Pinch of nutmege powder (Jaifal)
Oil for frying
For the Batter:

Gram flour (Vesan)—6-8 tbsp
Water—8 10 tbsps
Salt—1tsp
Green Chillies—1
Ginger—ground—one small piece.
Tymol seeds (Ajwain)—1/2 tsp.
Mint Chutney.

Clean and cut fish in big pieces. Sprinkle lime juice over the pieces. Apply dry ingredients over, set aside. Gradually add water to gram flour beating well to avoid lumps. Add salt, green chillies, ginger paste and tymol seeds. Set aside for 1 hour. Heat oil to smoking point. Dip fish in gram flour batter and fry to a crisp golden brown. Drain on absorbent paper. Serve hot with mint chutney.

19

Aloo Tikki (Fried Potato Cakes)

Potatoes—½ kg boiled and mashed
Bengal gram—½ cup
(Channa daal)
Cumin seed—½ tsp
Ginger—a small piece
Turmeric powder—¼ tsp
Salt to taste
Green chillies—2-3
Red Chillies—½ tsp
Chaat masala—1 tsp
Mixed spices (Garam masala)—½ tsp
Chopped corriander leaves—1 tsp
Ghee for shallow frying
Filling

Soak Bengal gram for two hours,, heat 1 tbsp oil or ghee in a pan—add Cuminseed, allow to splutter—Add chopped green chillies, red chillies and salt. Cover and let it cook on low heat till it is well cooked. Sprinkle water while cooking. It should be all dry. Add chaat masala—mixed spice and chopped coriander leaves. Allow it to cool.

Boil, peel and mash potatoes with a pinch of salt. Take a ball of mashed potatoes—oil palm slightly—make shallow cup with the ball of mashed potatoes, place a tea spoon of gram filling in centre and seal well and flatten the ball. Heat oil in a frying pan or grease the griddle shallow fry each tikki on low heat on both sides. Serve hot with mint chutney. Goes very well with khatte-chhole.

20

Mixed-Vegetable Tikki

Potato —1 kg.
Carrots—200 gms.
Peas--300 gms.
French Beans—150 gms,
Onion—1
Cauliflower—150 gms.
Ginger—100 gms.
Lemons—2
Green chillies—a few.
Cornflour—2 tbsp.
Gram Flour (roasted)—4 tbsp.
Chaat Masala—1 tbsp.
Mixed Spices—1 tsp.
(with nutmeg in it)
Oil or vanaspati ghee for frying.

Boil and mash potatoes. Chop and boil other vegetables. Chop onion, ginger and coriander leaves. Mix potatoes boiled vegetables—chopped onion, ginger and coriander. Add salt and green chillies and mixed spices.

Put Karahi on fire. Put the mixture in it and toss for two minutes. Remove from fire, add lemon juice, gram flour, cornflour and chaat masala. Make tikkis and shallow fry. Serve hot with (Pudina) mint chutney.

Ceresl Based Preparation

21

Dhingri-Chhole (Dried Mushrooms with White Gram)

> White grams—250 gms
> Dhingri—50 gms
> Onion—1
> Ginger—1 piece
> Garlic cloves—6-7
> Tomatoes—3 medium sized.
> salt—1 tsp.
> Red chilles (Whole)—5
> Turmeric powder—½ tsp
> Brown cardamom—2
> Cloves—4
> Cinnamon—1 stick.
> Coriander seed—1 tbsp.
> Cumin seed—1 tsp heaped
> Cooking oil—4 tbs
> Chopped coriander

Soak separately white gram and Dhingri overnight. Cut Dhingri in piece. Put tomatoes in boiling water, remove the skin and mash. Soak red chillies (removing seeds) in water. Grind onion garlic and ginger to a paste. Grind chillies and add to ginger-garlic paste.

Heat oil in a pan. When hot put cloves, cinnamon stick then add ground masala paste, salt and turmeric powder. Fry till it is brown and oil comes on top. Add tomato pulp. Lightly roast on girdle coriander seeds, cuminseeds and cardamom seeds. Cool and powder.

Add dhingri to the fried masala and lower the heat and slowly fry, sprinkling water. Add white grams and fry for another ten minutes on low heat. Add powdered dry masalas. Add enough water to cook the grams or pressure cook for 20 minutes. Serve garnished with chopped coriander.

Note : Dhingri can be cooked without grams. It makes an excellent dish for the vegetarians.

22

Khatte Chhole (Sour Grams)

White gram—250 gms.
Pinch of soda-bi-carb
Tea leaves—1 tbsp
Cardamom brown—4
Cinnamon—1 stick
Cloves—3
Cooking oil—1tbsp

Soak grams overnight with soda. Put the grams in pressure cooker with enough water, oil salt, cloves, cardamom and cinnamon. Put tea leaves in a small muslin cloth bag, tie it tightly and put in the cooker, with enough water to cook for 45 minutes.

Cooking oil—5 tbsp.
Pomegranate seeds—100 gms
(anardana).
Cuminseed—2 tbsp.
Onions chopped—4
Ginger—1" piece
Tomatoes chopped—4
Ginger—1" piece
Green chillies chopped—4
Turmeric powder—1 tsp

Coriander Powder—1 tsp
Red chillies—1 tsp
Salt to taste

Roast Pomegranate seeds and cuminseed on girddle (Tawa). When cool grind them to powder. Chop two onions, grind them. Heat some oil—fry the ground onions, add turmeric powder, coriander powder salt, keep aside. Chop the other 2 onions and ginger, fry a little, add chopped tomatoes, cook for 3—4 minutes, add cooked grams, removing the tea bag add the ground and fried onions—cook for a while. Add the pomegranate powder. If the grams are too dry add some water, let them simmer for some time, garnish with green chillies, tomato slices and onion rings—serve hot with Bhaturas or poories.

Note: Grams cooked in iron pan (Lohe-di-karahi) turn out tastier and darker in colour.

To make grams sour tamarind (soaked in water and mashed) pulp can be put instead of pomegranate seeds.

23

Shahi Kali Daal (Black Gram) (Maanh Sabat)

Sabat maanh (black gram)—250 gms
Garlic—1 pod
Ginger—1" Piece
Onion—1
Big tomatoes (soaked in warm water)—
Curd—125 gms
Salt—2 tsp
Red chillies—½ tsp
Pure ghee—2 tbsp
Mustard oil—1 tbsp
Pinch of asafoetida
(Turka—fry chopped onions, ginger and tomato—with
red chilli powder in pure Ghee)
Turka : Onion—1
ginger—1 small piece
tomato—1
Degi mirach—½ tsp
(red chillies)
Pure ghee—2 tbsp

Wash daal. Grind garlic, chop onion and grate ginger. Boil enough water in the pressure cooker, put daal and garlic ginger, onion, mustard oil in it with salt and chillies. Pressure cook for ½ hour. Open and add some hot water. Peel tomatoes, mash them, beat the curds, add to daal and cook for another 40 minutes. Open the cooker and stir well to mash the daal a bit, cook for 30 minutes more on slow fire. *Turka*: Chop 1 onion and ginger fry in pure ghee, and red chillies and chopped tomato, and pinch of asafoetida, fry. Pour it on the daal. While serving pour 1 tbsp hot pure ghee or fresh butter. Use Degi or Kashmiri mirach.

Note : Daal cooked in degkchi on slow fire for a few hours, tastes good and assimilates better. Put all the ingredients with lot of water in Degkchi and cover—cook for a few hours. Tomatoes and curds can be eliminated. Plain daal with turka tastes good.

Serve steaming hot daal with tandoori rotis and whole onions squashed and squeezed and green chillies.

24

Sukhi Urad Daal (Dry Pulse)

Urad washed—50 gms
Water—150 ml
Red chillies—½ tsp
Turmeric powder—1 tsp
Salt to taste
Garlic cloves—2-3 chopped
Small onion—½ chopped
Ginger—small piece finely chopped.
Cooking oil for turka—2 tbsp
Coriander chopped dry spices—1/2 tsp

Clean daal. Wash and soak in water and keep aside for about 15 minutes. Drain water and bring it to a boil, put daal in it and add salt, chillies dry ingredients and chopped onion, garlic, ginger. Add 1 tsp oil and let it cook when about to over boil slow the fire and half cover and let it cook till well cooked. Each grain of daal should remain separate and not become sticky. Cover and put it aside.

Turka : Chop one onion, 1″ piece ginger and tomato. Put oil in the frying pan and saute onions, add ginger and then tomatoes. Add ½ tsp mixed spices Heat the cooked daal, put it in a dish, heat turka and pour on it. Sprinkle chopped coriander and serve it hot.

25

Tari-wale-Rajmaanh (Kidney Beans in Gravy)

Kidney beans—250 gms
Onions—2
Garlic—8-10 Cloves
Ginger—1" piece
Tomatoes—2
Salt—1½ tsp
Turmeric powder—½ tsp
Red chillies ½ tsp
Cooking oil—3 tbsp
water—4 glasses
Chopped coriander

Wash and soak beans overnight. Grind onion, garlic and ginger. Soak tomatoes in hot water, remove the skin and mash. Heat oil in a pan, put ground masala and fry for 4-5 minutes, add salt, turmeric powder, chillies and mashed tomatoes. Fry on medium fire sprinkling water/occasionally. Fry till oil floats on top. Add kidney beans and fry for a few minutes. Add water and bring it to boil, let beans cook in it. When cooked, slow the heat and let it simmer for sometime. Add ground spices, some chopped coriander. Kidney beans when fully cooked burst and the gravy thickness slowly with it. If using pressure cooker, put four glasses of water. Pressure cook for 30 minutes, then lower the heat and cook for another 40 minutes. Cool, open the cooker and let it simmer on low heat for 15 minutes.

Serve with boiled rice or piaz-jeera pilauo.

Note: There are different varieties of kidney beans, small dark coloured ones from Jammu, dark big ones, and chitra. Chitra (Shaded) cook faster and better.

Vegetarian Preparations

Punjabis are equally fond of vegetarian food—that includes—all Daals—vegetables and panir preparations. Fresh vegetables are grown in Punjab round the year and Punjabi food includes lots of vegetables, preparations of peas, greens, brinjals, carrots, cauliflowers, lotus roots, jack fruit, lady fingers etc.

Mushrooms are considered the "Queen of Vegetables" and are a delight on the best tables in the world. Mushrooms were never a common man's diet. Earlier mushrooms were hand-picked from open wild places—now they are being cultivated and are easily available in season. Guchhi, dhingri and button mushrooms are gourmets' delight.

26. Sarson-da-saag
27. Punjabi malai palak
28. Dahi-karela
29. Lauki kofta
30. Mattar makhni
31. Bhartha
32. Masala baingan
33. Malai khumb
34. Dum aloo
35. Poori-wale-aloo
36. Sabat aloo
37. Aloo wadi
38. Sabat arbi
39. Masala gobhi.

Sarson-da-Saag (Mustard Greens)

Green mustard—1 kg.
Spinach or Baathoo—¼ kg
Onions—2
Garlic—1 pod
Ginger—50 gms
Salt to taste
Maize flour—1 tbsp
Turka:
Green chillies—4
Garlic—a few cloves
Onion—1
Ginger—1" piece
Chillies—2
Pure ghee—2 tbsp

Wash and clean mustard laves and spinach or baathoo. First remove hard big leaves, peel each stem. Then finely chop. Selection of saag is important. It should be with tender leaves and tender stems (gandal). Chop spinach or baathoo. Put it in a Degkchi with narrow mouth. Chop onions, garlic, ginger chillies, add to the saag, add salt and put it on fire and let it start heating. It will start going down. Cover and let it cook on medium fire or pressure cook for $\frac{1}{2}$ an hour. Remove from fire, add maize flour to the saag and grind it very well to a smooth paste. Cook for a few minutes. Chop onion, garlic and ginger, heat pure ghee, fry the chopped onions etc. Add cooked greens (saag) to it and toss.

Saag coocked a day earlier tastes better the next day. Served with fresh home made butter and Makki-di-Roti. (Maize Flour Roti)

This is real Punjab !

27

Punjabi Malai Palak (Cream Spinach)

Whole green gram (Sabat moong) 50 gms—
Spinach—500 gms
Green chilli—1 chopped
Ginger—$\frac{1}{2}''$ piece (shredded)
Turmeric powder —$\frac{1}{2}$ tsp
Onion—1 chopped
Salt—$1\frac{1}{2}$ tsp
Chilli powder—$\frac{1}{4}$ tsp
Well mixed curds—2 tbsps
Pinch of black pepper
Pure ghee—2 tbsps

Wash and remove thick stems and chop spinach and wash. Wash daal. In about 100 ml. water to which turmeric powder has been added, cook spinach daal-chilli and ginger, cook till it is thick and soft. Cool and grind it well.

Heat ghee, fry onion with chilli powder. Add spinach paste and salt, and fry for 3-4 minutes. Add well-mixed curds and black pepper. Add $\frac{1}{2}$ cup water and simmer till well-blended and the mixture is thick like cream.

28

Dahi-Karela (Bitter Gourd in Curds)

Karela—½ kg
Curds—6 tbsp
Onion (ground)—1 large
Garlic (ground)—½ pod
Tomato big-chopped and ground—1
Powdered coriander—1 tbsp
Red chilli powder— ½ tsp
Salt to taste
Oil for frying—4 tbsp.

Scrape the karelas, slit across, remove the seeds and make four pieces from each one. Sprinkle enough salt and put aside for 1 hour. Squeeze out the salted water from the Karelas, and wash. Soak in beaten curd for 20 minutes, (Keep 1 tbsp curd aside). Fry karelas on slow fire. Fry separately onion and garlic, add 1 tbsp curd, tomato pulp, salt and chillies and coriander powder. Add karelas to it and cook on slow fire.

29

Lauki Koftas (Green Gourd Balls)

Green gourd—$\frac{1}{2}$ kg
Gram flour—2 tbsp
Salt—1 tsp
Chaat masala—1/2 tsp
Soda—a small pinch
Mixed spices—1/2 tsp
Gravy: Oil for frying
Onions—2
Ginger—1″ piece.
Tomatoes—2
Salt—1$\frac{1}{2}$ tsp
Red chillies—to taste.
Turmeric powder—$\frac{3}{4}$ tsp.
Coriander leaves
Mixed spices (powder)
Cooking oil—3 tbsp.

Scrape and grate the gourd. Squeeze water and remove big seeds. Roast gram flour on (Tawa) girddle. Add gram flour and other dry ingredients to the grated gourd and mix. Make medium sized balls and deep fry in hot oil.

Similarly koftas can be made with lotus roots (Bhein, Kamal Kakri), wash and scrape 250 gms long lotus roots—grate them fine and add other dry ingredients, make balls and fry.

Gravy: Grate onion ginger and chop tomatoes. Put them in pressure cooker with half a cup of water. Steam for five minutes. Cool and open. Dry water and mash add, salt, turmeric powder, chillies and oil and fry the masala till it is golden and leaves the oil. Add water and make gravy, boil for five minutes. Heat the gravy, add koftas before serving. Garnish with coriander leaves.

30

Mattar Makhani (Butter Peas)

Shelled peas—2 cups
Coriander leaves—50 gms
Cuminseed—1 tsp
Salt—1½ tsp
Red chilli powder—½ tsp
Butter—2 tbsp
Cooking oil—1 tbsp
Melted butter—1 tbsp

Grind coriander leaves with sprinkling of water, when well ground, add more water and sieve. Heat oil, add cuminseed, let it splutter, add butter, salt and chillies and peas— Saute and add coriander water and cook till it is tender. Pour 1 tbsp, melted butter while serving.

Bhartha (Mashed Brinjal)

Round brinjals—$\frac{1}{2}$ kg
Onions—2
or spring onions—4
Tomato large—1
Ginger—1" piece
Coriander leaves chopped.
Salt to taste
Green chillies—2
Turmeric powder—$\frac{1}{4}$ tbsp
Pure Ghee—2 tbsp or
Cooking oil—4 tbsp

Roast the brinjals on open flame till the skin gets smoked and peels off. Put them in water and wash to remove the skin. Cut open the brinjals and remove the seeds. Mash them with wooden masher (madhana)—chop onions—ginger, tomatoes. Heat oil or ghee in Karahi, add them to it and saute for 3-4 minutes—add salt turmeric powder and the mashed brinjals and keep tossing gently. Let it cook on medium fire till ghee or oil appears on sides and add coriander leaves.

For Bhartha, quality of brinjals should be good, with less seeds and not hard tough brinjals. Bhartha cooked in pure ghee tastes much better.

32

Masala Baingan (Spicy brinjal)

Long brinjals—250 gms
Turmeric powder—1 tsp
Salt to taste—1 tsp
coriander seeds—2 tsp
Brown cardamom—2
Cuminseed—1 tsp
Pepper Corns—6
Red chillies—1/2 tsp
Potatoes large—2
Cooking oil—4 tbsp

Wash and wipe the brinjals and make four slits on each. **Peel** cut potatoes into long slices. Lightly roast coriander, cuminseed and cardamom seedon griddle. Add pepper corns and grind them together. Add salt turmeric powder and chillies. Mix the dry masala and fill the brinjals. Heat the oil in Karahi, add brinjals and potato slices and cook on medium fire. Cover the Karahi, sprinkle water and toss and cook till it is tender. Garnish with chopped coriander and serve.

33

Malai Khumb (Mushrooms-in-cream)

Mushrooms—250 gms
Cream—100 gms
Onion—1 large
Ginger —1 small piece
Tomato—1
Green chillies—2
Coriander leaves chopped
Oil or butter—1 tbsp
Vinegar—1 tsp.
Refined flour (maida)—1½ tsp
Cumminseed—1 tsp
Salt—1 tsp

Clean, wash and chop the mushrooms. Chop onion, ginger, tomato and chillies. Heat oil or butter in a pan, add flour, stir for a minute add cuminseed and chopped onion, ginger tomato and chillies and fry for 3—4 minutes. Add mushrooms vinegar and stir, cook on medium fire for a few minutes. Mushrooms cook fast. Add cream, (saving a little) and stir. Before serving pour the rest of the cream and garnish with coriander leaves. Mushrooms taste better when freshly cooked and served.

34

Dum Aloo (Whole Savoury Potatoes)

Small potatoes—½ kg
Onions—2
Cloves garlic—6
Ginger—1" piece
Cuminseed powder—2 tsp
Red chilli powder—1 tsp.
Garam Masala—2 tsp
Coriander Powder—1 tbsp
Curds—100 gms
Cooking oil—8 tbsp
Salt to taste

Peel the potatoes—prick with a fork and soak in salted water for one hour. Drain the potatoes. Heat the oil and fry them. Heat oil in dekchi, fry ground masala (onion, garlic, ginger ground together) add dry masala made from cuminseed to coriander powder. Add well beaten curds and potatoes and cook for 15 minutes. The potatoes should be cooked thoroughly. Serve garnished with fresh chopped coriander leaves.

Poori-wale-Aloo (Potatoes in Gravy)

Potatoes—500 gms
Tomatoes—250 gms
Cuminseed—1 tsp
Green chillies—3 chopped long pieces
Salt—2 tsp
Turmeric powder—1 tsp
Red chillies—½ tsp
Coriander leaves
Oil—4 tbsp
Water—4 cups (Approx.)

Boil, peel and cut the potatoes in pieces, soak tomatoes in hot water for a few minutes and peel off the skin and mash them. Heat oil in a pan, add cuminseed, turmeric powder, after a minute or two, add mashed tomatoes, salt and red and green chillies and fry for a few minutes. Add potatoes (keeping a handful aside) and toss for a couple of minutes. Add water and let it boil. Slow the fire and let it cook for two minutes for the gravy to thicken. Mash the potatoes and add to the gravy. Cook for another few minutes. Add chopped coriander and serve hot with pooris preferably.

Sabat Aloo (Whole Small Potatos with Jacket)

Very small potatoes—250 gms
Garlic—6-8 cloves
Ginger—1 small piece 2" long
Red chillies—½ tsp
Dry masala:
Cuminseed and Coriander—1tsp each lightly roasted and
powdered
Turmeric powder—½ tsp
Mustard oil—3 tbsp
Green coriander chopped
Red and green chillies—6

Wash the potatoes, prick with fork and dip in salted water.
Crush ginger and garlic together. Smoke oil in karahi. Add
ground ginger garlic paste, salt and turmeric. Add potatoes. Toss and turn. Add cuminseed and coriander powder. Cover, let it cook with steam. Sprinkle water as and
when required. Cut red and green chillies into two and add
to the potatoes before they are ready. Cover and cook. Add
chopped coriander leaves. Serve it hot.

Aloo-Wadi (Potatoes and Wadi Gravy)

Potatoes—$\frac{1}{2}$ kg
Tomatoes—2 chopped
Onion—1 sliced
Wadi—1
Turmeric powder—$\frac{3}{4}$ tsp
Salt to taste
Chilli powder—$\frac{1}{2}$ tsp
Cooking oil—4 tbsp

Boil, peel and cut the potatoes in pieces (not too small). Heat oil, add sliced onions and fry. Add tomatoes, salt, turmeric and chilli powder, add wadi broken into pieces and fry a bit, add potatoes and toss. Add 2 cups of water and let it cook till gravy is ready.

Note: Wadi is made from daal, flavoured with spices. It is dried in the sun and stored. Amritsar wadis are really exquisite.

Sabat Arbi (Whole Colocasia)

Colocasia—½ kg (medium size)
Garlic—½ pod
Large onion—chopped (long slices)
Tymol seeds (Aijwain)—1 tsp
Salt to taste
Chopped green chillies—2
Cooking oil—3 tbsp

Wash and scrape colocasia. Pound the garlic cloves. Heat oil—saute garlic, add tymol seeds—add scraped colocasia whole. Toss and turn, add salt and sliced onion. Cover and cook, sprinkle little water as and when needed. Do not let it become sticky, add chopped green chillies—toss and cover for further five minutes till it turns slightly golden in colour.

Serve it hot.

39

Masala Gobhi (Whole-Cauliflower)

Cauliflower medium—1
Big tomatoes—2
Large onions—2
Cloves garlic—6
Ginger—1" piece
Turmeric powder—½ tsp
Chilli powder—½ tsp
Salt to taste
Khaskhas—1 tbsp
Garam masala—2 tsp
Cooking oil—4 tbsp

Remove cauliflower leaves and wash the whole flower. Soak it in warm salted water for about 10 minutes. Then throw away the water and drain the water if any left in the cauliflower. Slice the onions—grind garlic and ginger, add khaskhas, grind it to a paste, add turmeric, garam masala, salt and chillies to it. Heat ghee in a Karahi, brown the onions, add the masala paste and fry for a few minutes, add chopped tomatoes and cook for 5-7 minutes. Then add the whole cauliflower and cook on slow fire till it is tender. Toss it gently till it is slightly browned. Garnish with chopped coriander and serve hot.

Masala Gobhi (Masala Cauliflower)

Medium size cauliflower
Cooking oil for frying
Onions—2
Tomatoes—4
Beaten curds—100 gms
Garlic—6 cloves
Ginger—small piece.

Soak gobhi in salted hot water. Heat oil and deep fry. Make onion masala, deep fry onions and grind well, add tomato puree and beaten curds—fry in oil. Grind garlic and ginger, add water and strain, add water of garlic and ginger—fry— add gobhi, simmer, for a few minutes, garnish with chopped coriander.

Note: For tomato puree soak tomatoes in hot water, remove the skin and mash them. .

Non-vegetarian Preparations

Non-vegetarian food holds a great fescination with the robust Punjabis. Food habits have been changing from Shudh-Vaishno (vegetarian) food to non-vegetarian food. With Muslim influence in the past, non-vegetarian food has become more popular. Even the climatic factor plays a vital role in winter and more meat diet is preferred. Chicken, mutton, fish and eggs make important part of non-vegetarian food in Punjabi homes.

40. Raada meat
41. Methi meat
42. Daal meat
43. Dahi meat
44. Hari tori meat
45. Chholia meat
46. Piaz-wala-meat
47. Tamatar chaamp
48. Murga masaledar
49. Murga makhani
50. Malai-wala-murga
51. Tandoori murga
52. Tari-wala-murga
53. Chandi chicken

40

Raada Meat

Mutton—1 kg
Curds—250 gms
Mutton mince keema—250 gms
Ginger paste—2" piece
Garlic cloves— 1 pod
Coriander seeds—1 tbsp
Onions—4
Cloves—4
Brown cardamom---4
Red chillies—3
Salt—3 tsp
Mixed spices—1 tsp
Cooking oil—6 tbsp

Wash and clean mutton. Beat curds, add salt, mutton and keema. Marinate for half an hour. Put the pan on medium heat and cook for an hour, then dry the water and roast mutton on medium heat. Make paste with garlic and ginger—heat oil in a pan—put cloves and broken cardamoms and ginger garlic paste and fry it light brown. Chop onions and fry them brown—take them out of the pan and grind them with red chillies. Keep it aside.

Add cooked mutton to fried garlic paste, fry for a few minutes, add 750 ml. water and let it cook on medium fire till mutton is tender. Add onion paste and fry till oil leaves the masala. Sprinkle mixed spices. Serve it garnished with chopped coriander.

41

Methi Meat (Mutton in Fenugreek)

Mutton—$\frac{1}{2}$ kg
Fenugreek—$\frac{1}{2}$ kg
Large onion—1
Ginger—1" piece
Garlic cloves—5-6
Large tomato—1
Cumin seed—$\frac{1}{2}$ tsp
Coriander seed—$\frac{1}{2}$ tsp
Salt—1 tsp
Turmeric powder—$\frac{1}{2}$ tsp
Red chillies—$\frac{1}{2}$ tsp
Mixed dry spices—$\frac{1}{2}$ tsp
Curds—1 cup
Water—2 cups
Cooking oil—4-5 tsps

Remove the stems of fenugreek and chop, put salt and leave it aside and let the water drain out. Then wash it thoroughly.

Beat the curds, marinate mutton in it with chopped fenugreek and salt and keep it aside for two hours. Make masala paste with onion-ginger and garlic (grind them together). Heat oil in a pan and fry the masala. Make tomato puree, dip tomato in hot water, remove the skin and mash. Add it to the masala. Fry till the oil separates from the masala. Add marinated mutton and dry spices—(grind cuminseed and coriander seed together) and red chillies, fry till oil separates. Add water and cook till the meat is tender—dry the water—add mixed spice. Serve with plain pranthas.

And watch the eaters !

42

Daal Meat (Mutton Cooked in Pulse)

[Channa (Bengal gram) daal—170 gms. soaked in sufficient water for 2 hours and drained.]

Mutton pieces—400 gms
Large onion—1
Garlic cloves—4
Ginger pieces—½"
Red chillies —2
Green cardamoms—2
Cloves pounded—2
Bay leaves—2
Turmeric powder—½ tsp
Salt—2 tsp
Oil—3 tbsp
Curds—3 tbsp
Water for cooking daal and meat separately.

Cook daal in water until it is almost tender. Set it aside. Grind to paste onions, garlic and ginger. Heat oil, add ground paste, red chillies—turmeric powder and meat—fry with a sprinkling of water until it turns golden brown, add bay leaves cardamoms, salt, cloves and curds, cook further until the aroma of the curds is absorbed by the meat. Add water about $\frac{1}{2}$ litre. Cover and cook until meat is tender and almost dry. Now mix in daal, add 1/2 cup of water, cover and simmer until well-blended. It is dry form of daal. Sprinkle $\frac{1}{2}$ tsp of garam masala (mixed spices).

Dahi Meat (Mutton in Curds)

Mutton—1 kg
Onion—5
Garlic—10 cloves
Ginger—1" piece
Curds—250 gms
Garam masala—2 tsp
Salt—2 tsp
Red chillies—1 tsp
Turmeric powder—1/2 tsp
Cooking oil

Beat curds—soak mutton with garam masala in curds. Keep it aside for a few hours.

Chop the onions, grind to a fine paste, along/with garlic and ginger. Fry the ground masala till, it is pale brown add marinated meat to it—add salt, turmeric powder and red chillies. Pressure cook for about 10 minutes or till cooked, dry the water and roast till oil leaves the side of the pan. Garnish with chopped coriander leaves. Serve it hot.

44

Hari Tori Meat (Mutton in Ridge Gourd)

Meat cut into pieces—1/2 kg
Ridge gourd—1/2 kg
Spices
Green chillies—2
Cloves—4
Cardamom green—3
Garlic cloves—6-8 cloves
Ginger—1" piece
Cuminseed—1 tsp
Onions—3
Grate and grind the onions
Beaten curds—6 tbsp
Cooking Oil

Scrape and chop ridge gourd—put it in a pan and let it cook a while to dry out its extra water.

Heat oil and fry light brown the ground onions—add ginger and garlic paste. Add cloves—cardamom, cuminseed salt and chillies. Cook till masala leaves the oil—add curds, let it mix with the masala—add meat pieces—fry it a little. Pressure cook for 10 minutes—then add ridge gourd. Cook for five minutes—dry the excess water and serve hot.

Chholia Meat (Green-Gram in Mutton)

Shelled green gram—250 gms
Mutton—750 gms
Onions—4
Garlic—1 pod
Ginger—25 gms. ground to a paste
Tomatoes—4
Salt—2 tsp
Red chillies—$\frac{3}{4}$ tsp
Turmeric powder—1 tsp
Mixed spices—1 tsp
Curds—2 tbsp
Coriander leaves chopped
Cooking oil—6 tbsp
Water—2 cups

Wash and wipe mutton pieces. Heat oil, fry onion garlic ginger paste and salt chillies, turmeric powder. Keep stirring adding beaten curds and water. Add tomatoes fry till oil separates from the masala, add meat and fry further for five minutes—add shelled green grams, add water. Pressure cook for 10-15 minutes—remove from fire, let it cook, open and dry extra water—add mixed spices, garnish with coriander leaves.

Piazwala Meat (Mutton in Onions)

Mutton (tender cut)—750 gms
Beaten curds—6 tbsps
Onions sliced—4
Ginger finely sliced—1"
Garlic chopped—6 cloves
Cardamoms green—6
Bay leaves—2
Cinnamon stick—1"
Cloves—4
Pepper corns—10
Cumin seeds—1 to 1½ tbsp
Small red chillies—6
Salt—2 tsp
Cooking oil—6-8 tbsp
Almonds—12-blanched and sliced
Coriander leaves chopped

Heat cooking oil and fry three sliced onions. Remove from oil and *crush*. Wash and dry the mutton pieces. In the same oil put mutton and all the ingredients except the fried onions, almonds and chopped coriander. Put ½ cup of water and pressure cook for 10 minutes. Add the crushed onions and sliced almonds, cook for a few minutes on slow fire. Lift from heat, serve hot garnished with chopped coriander leaves. Best eaten with phulka or prantha.

Tamatar Chaamp (Mutton Tomato Chops)

Mutton chops—1 kg
Large onions—3
Tomatoes—500 gms blanched and pureed
Onions—3 sliced
Garlic cloves—10
Ginger—1 piece (grind to paste)
Red chillies—2
Salt—2 tsp
Cloves—6
Cardamoms green—6
Cinnamon—1" stick
Cumin seeds— 1½ tsps
Red chillies—3
Cooking oil—6 tbsps
Coriander leaves

Clean and wash the chops. Heat oil. Add onion slices and whole spices. Saute for 5 minutes. Add chops and salt. Simmer with a sprinkling of water till the meat is almost tender. Remove from pan. In the same oil fry ground paste till it turns golden brown in colour. Add pureed tomatoes and red chillies and cook it stirring until the gravy is thick and creamy. Add cooked chops and 2 cups of hot water. Simmer for another 10 to 15 minutes until the gravy is well blended and the chops are tender and add more water if required. Garnish with coriander leaves.

Murga Makhani (Butter Chicken)

Chicken—750-1000 gms—cut into pieces
To marinate the chicken—
Ginger—1" piece⎤
Garlic—6 cloves ⎬*grind together*
Onion—1 ⎦
Lemon juice—2 tsp
Salt—½ tsp
Coriander powder—1 tsp
Cuminseed powder—½ tsp
Cooking oil—1 tbsp
Vinegar—1 desert spoon
Chillies—¾ tsp
Edible orange colour a few drops
For sauce
Butter—50 gms
Red chillies—1 tsp
Tomatoes—½ kg
Salt—2 tsp
Sugar—3-4 tsp
Thick cream—50 gms
Oil—4 tbsp
Small piece shredded ginger

Finely cut chillies—2-3

Tomatoes cut into bits—2

To sprinkle on top

Dried methi powder—½ tsp

Cuminseed powder—½ tsp

Coriander powder—½ tsp

Dry mango powder (amchoor)—½ tsp

Butter melted—50 gms

Marinate the chicken in the given ingredients for a few hours.

To make sauce. Heat butter, remove from fire, add 1 tsp red chillies ½ kg roughly cut tomatoes, salt, sugar, cook uncovered on hot fire till the puree thickens and add well beaten cream. Remove from fire. Cover till required. (Or soak tomatoes in hot water, peel and mash them to make pulp and cook with other ingredients.)

Cook the marinated chicken till it is almost done—then fry it in oil or butter—remove from fire add ½ tsp red chillies, add the prepared puree to it—cook for 5 minutes, add bits of tomatoes, bits of ginger and chillies—simmer for 7 minutes. Melt 50 gms butter, pour over chicken after putting the chicken in the dish sprinkle—roasted cuminseed powder and mixed spices, coriander powder, dried fenugreek, dried mango powder (mixed together ½ tsp each).

49

Murga Masaledar (Masala Chicken)

One medium sized chicken

> Onions—3
> Garlic—1/2 pod
> Ginger—1" piece
> Coriander seeds—6 tsp
> Cuminseed—2 tsp
> Cardamoms—6 big
> Cloves—6
> Cinnamon—2 pieces
> Sugar—1 tsp.
> Tomatoes—2
> Green chillies—5
> Cooking oil—4 tbsp.
> Turmeric powder—1 tsp
> Salt, red chilli powder to taste
> Grind to a paste
> 1. Onion separately
> 2. Ginger and garlic together
> 3. Coriander and cuminseed together
> 4. Cardamom, cloves and cinnamon together.

Cut the chicken into pieces. Pour oil in degkchi, let it heat, add sugar and brown. Now add ground onions and cook till they are of a dark brown colour. Add ginger garlic paste. Mix well and add garam masala paste and after stirring, add the coriander cuminseed paste. Cook the masala for a minute. Add chicken pieces, salt, chilli, powder and turmeric powder. Mix it well, fry the chicken well till oil comes out. Add two cups of warm water, green chillies and tomatoes cut in pieces and let it cook on slow fire for about half an hour or pressure cook for about 10 minutes. Sprinkle green coriander on the chicken pieces before serving.

50

Malaiwala Murga (Sour Cream Chicken)

Broiler—750 gms
Cream—200 gms, ½ cup curds
Cashew nuts—15-20
Onions—2 chopped
Tomatoes—3 chopped
Salt—1 tsp
Red chillies—½ tsp
Mixed spices—1½ tsp
Coriander leaves
Oil—4 tbsp

Heat oil, fry onions, add tomatoes, salt, chillies, 1 tsp mixed spices and chicken pieces. Keep on frying for 5-10 minutes. Put it on slow fire with sprinkling of water till it is almost done.

Beat curds and add to the cream. Grind cashewnuts, add sour cream and add it to the cooked chicken—cook on slow fire, add ½ tsp spices. Remove from fire. Serve garnished with chopped coriander leaves.

Tandoori Murga (Chicken Tandoori)

Chicken—750 gms
Garlic—½ pod
Ginger—½" piece
Small onion—1
Lemon juice—½ tsp
Cuminseed powder—1 tsp
Coriander powder—1 tsp
Beaten curds—1 cup
Cooking oil—2 tbsp
Orange colour—a few drops
Fenugreek powder (Dried methi)—1 tsp
Dried mango powder (amchoor)—½ tsp
Slices of lemon and onion rings to garnish

Clean the chicken. Prick it nicely with fork. Make paste with ginger garlic and onion—add salt, chilli powder, cumin powder, coriander powder, lemon juice to it and mix the paste into the well beaten curds, add colour to it and mix well. Add chicken pieces to it and keep it for 4-6 hours to marinate. Heat the oven to 425 F Put the chicken with the marinade in a dish and cook in the oven for about 15 minutes, when it is nearly done pour oil on it. Mix together garam masala, methi and amchoor and sprinkle all over the chicken—keep in the oven for another five minutes. Serve with slices of lemon and onion rings.

Tandoor: Put marinated chicken on skewer and leave it in the hot tandoor and keep turning till it is tender and roasted evenly. Rub little oil in it, sprinkle dry masalas and serve it hot.

Tariwala-Murga (Chicken in Curry)

Chicken (preferably desi)—1 kg.
Onion—2 chopped
Garlic—8-10 cloves
Ginger—1 small piece
Tomato—2 large
Salt—1½ tsp
Turmeric powder—¾ tsp
Red chillies—½ tsp
Mixed spices—1 tsp
Butter—3-4 tbsp
Coriander leaves—chopped

Cut chicken into pieces. Heat butter in degkchi—(pan) add chopped onion—pounded garlic and ginger—fry a little, add chopped and mashed tomatoes and dry ingredients. Add chicken pieces and toss it all. Let it cook on slow fire stirring often, sprinkle water to avoid smoking. Chicken will cook along with masala. When chicken is cooked add 3 cups of water and bring it to boil—slow the heat—let it simmer for the gravy to absorb the flavour. Serve hot garnished with coriander leaves.

Goes well with Tandoori Roti.

53

Chandi Chicken

Chicken—1 kg cut it into medium sized pieces
Curds—250 gms
Vinegar—2 tbsp
Large onions—2 grated
Red chillies—4
Garlic—10 cloves   grind together
Ginger—1" piece
Turmeric powder—1½ tsp
Coriander powder—1 tbsp
Cuminseed powder—1 tbsp
Pepper—½ tsp
Onions—3 finely chopped
Mixed spices—1 tbsp
Salt—2 tsp
Ghee—½ cup
Cooking oil—½ cup
Fresh khoya—250 gms

Heat 1 tbsp oil and fry khoya till it is brown, set it aside.

Marinate the chicken for two hours in curds along with other ingredients (except the chopped onions and mixed species). Heat oil in a degkchi. When properly heated add half the ghee and fry chopped onions to a crisp brown. The add the marinated chicken with masalas etc. Fry for five minutes. Cover the 'Degkchi' and cook till the chicken is tender—stirring from time to time. Add fried khoya and stir it well. If there is gravy, cook on slow fire till it is dry. Then add the rest of the ghee and mixed spices after taking off the fire. Garnish with silver foil (varq). Serve with pranathas.

Fish

In Punjab fresh water fish from rivers and lakes is obtained. Fish is a rich protein diet and is easy to digest. Rahu is the popularly eaten fish. Careful selection is needed to ensure it is fresh. For Punjabi style cooking apply wheat flour or (vesan) gram flour batter all over the fish. Keep aside for 5-10 minutes-wash thoroughly in cold water. Lime and salt also serve the purpose of taking away the fishy smell. Sea fish is also eaten wherever it is available.

54. Tandoori Fish
55. Punjabi Fried Fish
56. Fish Tikki

Tandoori Fish

Saul, Pomfret or any fish without small bones—750 gms
For the Marinade
Cumin seeds—1 tsp
Garlic—4 cloves
A large piece of ginger
Big pinch of (ajwain)—tymol seeds
Red chillies—2
Curds—2 tbsp
(Amchoor) dried mango powder—½ tsp
Tomato ketchup—½ tbsp
Oil—1 tbsp
Black pepper powder—¼ tsp
Lime juice—2 tsp
Oil—1 tbsp
Dried crushed fenugreek (Methi)
for sprinkling on top ½ tsp

Clean the fish. Remove head, tail and skin. Make gashes in the fish. Grind cumin seeds, garlic, ginger tymol seeds (ajwain) and red chillies. Rub this paste on the fish alongwith beaten curds, amchoor (mango powder), ketchup, salt, and oil. Put it aside for two hours. Pierce a skewer lengthwise through the fish and bake in a tandoor or over charcoal fire. It can also be done under an electric grill. Cooking does not take more than 10 to 15 minutes. Paste with the spicy sauce. Sprinkle methi before serving. Goes well with pickled small onions.

Panjabi Tali Machhi (Punjabi Fried Fish)

> Fish — 500 gms
> Onion — 100 gms
> Ginger — 5 gms   ⎫
> Garlic cloves — 3-4   ⎬ (Grind together)
>   ⎭
> Ground cuminseed — 1 tsp
> Turmeric — 1½ tsp
> Chillie powder — 1 tsp
> Salt — 1 tsp
> Mango powder — 1 tsp
> Mixed dry spices — 1 tsp
> Oil for frying

Clean the fish and remove the bones. Wash well. Cut into 3″ pieces. In the ground masala, add dry ingredients and smear all over the fish pieces. Set aside for about 3 hours. Deep fry lightly in hot oil. Keep aside. When about to serve—deep fry again. Serve with mint chutney.

56

Fish Tikkis

Minced fish—½ kg
Bengal gram (Channa daal)—1 cup
Garlic—1 pod
Onion—1 (small) chopped finely
Pomegranate seeds—1 tsp pounded
Tymol (ajwain) seed—½ tsp
Salt to taste
Green chillies—2 chopped
Green coriander—chopped
Oil for frying

Mince the fish pieces (without bones). Wash and soak daal, boil till it is cooked. Pound daal add, to the minced fish. Add all other ingredients. Heat oil in the frying pan. Make flat tikkis on the palm and fry or make balls and fry. Serve hot with mint chutney.

The Bread Basket

(Roti-Phulka)

Dough. *Sieve the flour-knead with water to a smooth dough. Keep it aside. Prepare the dough a couple of hours in advance. It makes better roties. Roll out small balls of dough on rolling board with rolling pin-using flour. Heat griddle (tawa) and cook the roti on both sides and put on apen flame. It puffs up like a balloon. Smear phulka with butter or pure ghee for added flavour. Plain phulka making needs more practice though it is simple to make.*

Roti is thicker than phulka and it does not puff up.

Plain rotis (phulkas) made with wheat flour are popular with each meal.

57. Missi roti
58. Pudina roti
59. Methi-wali-roti
60. Stuffed pranthas
61. Makki-di-roti
62. Mithi roti
63. Choori
64. Bhaturas

Missi Roti (Wheat and Gram Flour Roti)

Gram flour—250gms
Wheat flour—1kg
Salt—2tsp
Red chillies—1tsp
Chopped onion—1
(Tymol seeds Aijwain)—1tsp
Pomegranate seeds (Anardana)—1tsp-well pounded
Oil or ghee
Fresh butter or pure ghee
curds

Sieve and knead gram and wheat flour to a smooth dough.
Add all other ingredients—shape into balls. Roll out each
ball, put little ghee and roll again. Cook it on hot tawa, when
half done, roast it on either side on open fire. Butter it nicely
or even pure ghee can be used. Serve with fresh butter and
curds and mangoes in summer. Tomato or mango chutney
goes well with it.

Note : Butter milk (Lassi) and Missi roti go very well too.

58

Pudina Roti

Wheat flour dough
Pure Ghee
Dried crushed mint leaves

Take a ball of the dough and roll it out on the rolling board. Apply some ghee and fold it up—roll and twist it in circular way and roll it out again. Rolling and twisting will make folds in the roti. Put it on hot tawa and half bake on both sides. Roast on the flame, apply ghee and sprinkle crushed mint leaves and fold up the roti, serve it hot. Goes well with daal and meat dishes.

Methiwali-Roti (Fenugreek Roti)

Maize flour—½ kg
Fenugreek fresh-green—250 gms
Onion-finely chopped—1
Green chillies chopped—2
Salt to taste
Hot water to knead the flour
Oil to fry the roti

Sieve the flour-wash, remove the stems and chop fenugreek leaves. Mix the chopped fenugreek leaves in the flour, add salt, chopped onions and green chillies. Knead the flour with hot water. Knead to a smooth dough. Heat the Tawa (griddle). Take a ball of the dough. Put flour on the rolling board—and flatten the ball with the palm. Put it on the hot griddle and cook on both sides, and fry the roti like prantha. Serve hot with curds and cream (malai).

Stuffed Paranthas

[Stuffing—Cauliflower—Radish—Potato or Peas.]

Wheat flour —½ kg
Cauliflower—1 medium size
Cooking oil or vanaspati ghee for frying
Salt to taste
Red chilli powder—½ tsp
Chaat Masala—1tsp
Mixed spices—1tsp
Green chillies chopped—3
Coriander leaves chopped
Chopped onion—1
Ginger grated
Tymol seeds—½ tsp
Pomegranate seeds—1 tsp pounded

Sieve and knead the flour to smooth dough and keep it aside. Remove stems and leaves, wash the cauliflower. Grate or chop finely. Add chopped onions-ginger and dry masalas, all the ingredients.

Roll out two small balls of flour—put about 1½ tbsp cauliflower filling on one and put the other on top and seal the edges and roll out gently. Put griddle (tawa) on fire when it is hot, put rolled out prantha on it and let it cook—fry with ghee or oil on both sides.

Serve with fresh butter and curds. Mango chutney goes well with these.

Variations in prantha stuffing

Boil potatoes, peel and mash, add all the ingredients as mentioned and use the stuffing in pranthas.

Wash, scrape and grate radish. Squeeze out water—add the other ingredients.

Pound nicely fresh peas and add other ingredients.

Fenugreek leaves: Wash and grind fenugreek leaves. Suqeeze if there is extra water. Mix it in the dough, add salt red chillies, chopped onions—ginger and green chillies. Roll out the dough ball and cook the prantha—fry in ghee.

Makki-di-Roti.

Maize flour (from corn)
Hot water
Ghee for frying

Sieve the flour. Knead it with hot water slowly and keep kneading till the dough is soft and smooth.

Put some flour on a flat base—'Chakla'. Take a ball of the dough—put some flour on the palm and spread it with the palm slowly on the rolling board. Gently lift it and put it on hot tawa—on the fire, and let one side cook, then cook the other side. Put ghee and fry it and serve hot with saag or jaggery and pure ghee (Ghee-Shakkar). Roti can be roasted on the flame and served smeared with pure ghee or butter.

Note : Makki-di-Roti and Sarson-da-Saag is the most popular combination in Punjabi food.

Ghee Shakkar (Jaggery and Pure Ghee)
Pure ghee—2 tbsps
Shakkar—4 tbsps

Heat ghee, add shakkar to it. Mix well and serve it hot.

62

Mithi Roti (Sweet Roti)

Wheat flour—1 kg
Sugar or jaggery—½ kg
Aniseed (saunf)—3 tsps.
Oil or ghee for frying

Sieve and knead the flour to smooth dough. Roll out a ball of dough. Spread oil, 2 tsp sugar and a big pinch of aniseed. Roll it up and roll out again a bit thick. Cook on hot tawa on both sides, fry with ghee or oil.

63

Choori

Wheat flour roti—1
Pure ghee—1½ tbsp
Sugar—1½ tbsp

Take hot roti nicely roasted, crumble it with hands—add hot ghee and sugar and mix it. Serve it hot. It tastes delicious and is nourishing. Choori is the chaser to Neem ras, given in summer as a blood purifier.

Note : Make thick roti for making choori.

64

Bhaturas

Flour—250 gms
Soda-bi-carb —½ tsp
Curds—5 tbsp
Sugar—1 tbsp
Salt—1 tbsp
Ghee or oil—2 tbsp
Water—60 ml
Ghee or oil for frying

Mix two tbsp curds add sugar, salt, soda, one tbsp ghee and 2 tbsp flour. Mix well. Sprinkle with a tbsp water. Keep covered with damp cloth for a few hours for the paste to ferment. Add the paste to the flour and curds mixing well gradually. Add water kneading and stretching to a soft consistency dough. Cover with muslin cloth rinsed out in hot water. Keep in a warm place for 3-4 hours. Make balls the size of a golf ball—roll out on palms. Deep fry in boiling hot oil.

Bhaturas go very well with khatte-chhole.

Rice Pilau

Wheat is the staple food of Punjab. Punjabis are not rice eaters. Wheat flour is a source of energy. Daal Roti makes a common meal for Punjabis.

65. Guchhi pilau
66. Panir pilau
67. Methi-panir pilau
68. Wadi pilau
69. Mitha gajar pilau
70. Mithe chawal
71. Gur wale chawal

65

Guchhi Pilau

Guchhis—50 gms
Rice—2 cup
Water—4 cup
Onion—1
Cloves—4
Brown cardamom—3 lightly pounded
Bay leaf—3
Cooking oil—4 table spoon
Salt—2 tea spoon

Wash the guchhis thoroughly after taking out their stems, till they are rid of dust, which they accumulate in plenty. Soak them at night. Fry them in one table spoon oil and cook in little water till they are tender.

Soak rice in four cups of water for 15 minutes before cooking.

Slice the onion. Heat oil in a pan, fry onions light brown. Put salt and whole/dry masalas in it. Add rice and lightly fry them. Add cooked guchhis and fry a little.

Add water and cook by covering the pan. When the water gets absorbed-lower the heat and put some weight on the lid and let the rice cook fully and serve hot, garnished with fried onion slices.

66

Panir Pilau

Basmati rice—250 gms
Salt—1 tsp.
Green and yellow colouring
Panir made from 1 litre fresh milk
cut into neat 1" square pieces
Flour—2 tbsp
Salt—$\frac{1}{4}$ tsp
Pepper—$\frac{1}{2}$ tsp
Pinch of red chillies
Mix flour and other ingredients with
little water to a paste
Curds—4 tbsp
A pinch of saffron (Kesar)
Green cardamoms—seeds curshed—2
6 drops of yellow colouring
Cooked peas—1 cup
Pure ghee—1 tbsp
1" piece ginger, thinly sliced onions—2 thinly sliced
Cloves of garlic—10 finely chopped
Onions thinly sliced—$\frac{3}{4}$ cup
Red chillies—1 tsp

To garnish : Garam masala—1 tsp
Cuminseed 1 tsp
Sliced cucumber—1
Fresh coriander leaves chopped

Boil rice with 1 tsp salt and divide rice into two parts. Sprinkle 4 drops of yellow colour—in a little water and mix well, add it to one part of the rice, colour the other half green with 6 drops of green colour in 1 tbsp of water.

Fry the panir in oil with the batter of flour. Dip each cube in the batter and deep fry in hot oil.

1. Fry the onion and ginger lightly. Keep it aside. Dissolve saffron in a little water, add powdered green cardamom, add the whipped curd to the cardamom paste and a bit of yellow colouring. After this soak panir in the curd saffron mixture.

2. Fry rest of the onions and ginger and garlic, when it is light brown add the peas. Grease a dish—put a layer of yellow rice on the bottom, sprinkle little garam masala—red chillies and put a layer of panir cubes, fried onions and ginger and half of the green rice. Put a layer of peas remaining half of green rice and sprinkle garam-masala-cumin seeds—chillies. Press it down firmly. Pour over it 2 tbsps of melted ghee Cover it and bake it in the oven at 350—for half an hour. Take it out on a flat dish garnish with cucumber slices, fresh coriander leaves or serve from the dish only.

Methi Panir Pilau (Fresh Fenugreek and Cheese rice)

Fresh fenugreek—125 gms.
Cottage cheese from—½ kg milk
Rice basmati—250 gms (Soak in double quantity water)
Oil for frying and cooking rice
Salt—1 tsp
Turmeric powder—1/2 tsp

Wash, remove the stems, and boil fenugreek. Make panir, cut into pieces and fry. When fenugreek is cooked grind to fine paste.

Heat oil in the pan, add fenugreek and add turmeric powder cottage cheese and fry. Add soaked rice, fry a bit add water and cook like any other rice pilau.

Wadi Pilau

Rice—1 cup
Water—2 cups
Salt—1 tsp
Turmeric powder—½ tsp
Cuminseed—½ tsp
Wadi (broken into peices)—½
Cooking Oil—2 tbsp

Wash and soak rice in 2 cups of water. Heat oil, add wadi pieces, cuminseed—turmeric powder and salt, fry. Add water from the soaked rice. Let it boil, add the rice cover and let the rice cook. When the water is absorbed by the rice slow the fire, put weight on the lid and make the pan air tight, let the rice cook. Serve it hot.

Mitha Gajar Pilau (Sweet-Carrot-Rice)

Rice—1 cup
Sugar—1 cup
Water/for rice—2 cups
Water for sugar syrup—$\frac{1}{2}$ cup
Carrots grated—$\frac{3}{4}$ cup
Ghee or C. oil—2 tbsp
Edible colour—Yellow
Almonds—10

Wash and soak rice in 2 cups of water. Heat oil—Saute rice add water and colour—let it boil and cook.

Put 1 tsp sugar and carrots together in a pan to dry the water. Make syrup with water and sugar.

When rice is almost cooked add sugar syrup and carrots. Turn with the back of a spoon and cook till syrup is absorbed fully.

Serve hot garnished with blanched sliced almonds.

Mithe Chawal (Sweet Rice)

Rice—1 cup
Sugar—170 gms
Juice of one orange
Cinnamon—2 sticks—broken into pieces
Cardamom Green—4
A pinch of saffron—soaked in 2-3 tbsp warm milk
2-3 drops of edible yellow colouring
Shredded orange peel—1 tbsp
Almonds—30 blanched and chopped
Cooking oil—4 tbsp
Water to make syrup—1 cup
Silver foil to garnish

Wash the rice. Par boil in plenty of fast boiling water. Drain and rinse in cold water and spread in a thali at once. Boil the water, add sugar and cook till the sugar dissolves and is almost one—thread consistency. Remove from heat. Heat oil—fry cardamom and cinnamon and par boiled rice, syrup, orange juice, peel and saffron. Cover and cook over low heat, placing tawa under the pan till the rice is tender and fluffy. Remove from heat, mix in some almonds, serve decorated with silver foil and remaining almonds.

71

Gur wale Chawal

Rice 1 cup—100 gms.
Gur—200 gms. equal weight (Wash and soak rice in water)
Cooking oil—3 tbsp
Cuminseed—1 tsp
Brown cardamom—2 (Broken)
(Saunf) Aniseed—1 tsp
Orange juice—½ cup
Dried orange peel a few bits
Raising, almonds, dry coconut

In 1/4 cup water dissolve the pounded gur and keep it aside. Heat oil in a pan—add dry spices, saute for a while, add one cup of water, add rice, orange peel and orange juice. Heat gur soaked in water. When rice is nearly cooked add gur syrup and cook on slow fire. Add raisins. Let the syrup be fully absorbed and rice fully cooked. Serve hot. Garnish with blanched almonds and grated coconut. Serve it with fresh cream.

Desserts and Mithais

Punjabis have rather sweet teeth. Sweet-dish is a must after each meal followed by Gur as a digestive. Doctors' warnings against diabetes are thrown to the winds.

72. Halwa
73. Gajrela
74. Phirni
75. Rice kheer
76. Phenian-di-kheer
77. Ghia-di-kheer
78. Rauh-di-kheer
79. Gajar-di-kheer
80. Mal poora
81. Rabri
82. Kulfi Mithais

Mithais :
83. Bhugga
84. Pinni-maah-di-daal-di
85. Suji-di-pinni
86. Jalebi
87. Gulab jamun
88. Shkkar-paare
89. Balu shahi
90. Panjiri
91. Vesan-di-Barfi
92. Akhrot-in-gur

72

Halwa (Kadah)

Semolina—1 cup
Sugar—1 cup
Pure ghee—1 cup
Water—4 cups
Mixed dry fruit (almonds, dry coconut, raisins—25 gms)

Mix sugar and water and boil to make syrup—keep aside.
Heat ghee in karahi and fry sieved semolina in it till, it is
golden brown. Add the sugar syrup stirring constantly to
avoid lumps. Cook till water is absorbed. Add dry fruit. Use
some to garnish. Serve it hot. It makes a good combination
with poori (Halwa Poori).

For 1 cup wheat flour—use 2 cups water.

For 1 cup Gram flour—use 1 cup water.

Halwa can be made with semolina, wheat flour or gram
flour.

73

Gajrela (Carrot Halwa)

Carrots—1 kg
Sugar—400 gms
Water—2 cups
Milk—1kg
Almonds—10-12
Pistachio (Pista)—10
Pure ghee—2 tbsp
Silver foil—to decorate
Khoya—100 gms

Wash the carrots and scrape off the skin. Grate them fine, add milk to the grated carrots and cook on slow fire till the mixture becomes dry. Mix the sugar and water in another pan and cook on a slow fire till the sugar dissolves. Increase the heat and bring to boil, fast cook the syrup till it forms a single thread. Add the cooked carrots and ghee to the syrup and continue cooking on a slow fire. In the meantime blanch and slice the almonds and slice pistachio. Fry halwa till it leaves the sides of the pan. Add crumbled khoya to the halwa-add some sliced almonds and pista. Serve hot, garnish with almonds and pista and silver foil.

Note: Carrots can be cooked in cream removed from boiled and cooled milk. For 1 kg carrots—250 gms cream with some milk will do. Add sugar to taste.

Phirni (Rice Flour Cream)

Milk—1 kg
Rice—5tbsp
Sugar—100 gms (approx)
Green Cardamom (powdered)—2
Chopped almonds—6
Pistachio sliced—6
Saffron—a pinch
Silver foil (Varq)

Soak saffron in little water and keep it aside.

Soak rice in water for one hour and grind to a fine paste adding little water. Heat milk and let it boil for 5—10 minutes, lower the heat, add rice paste stirring constantly. Or boil milk for five minutes. Keep ½ cup cold milk aside. Make thin paste of rice powder with some cold milk and slowly add to the boiling milk. Keep stirring. Do this on slow fire, keep stirring till it thickens—add sugar stir and take off from fire—add saffron and cardamom powder. Put it in a bowl and let it cool-chill-garnish with almonds and pistachio.

This can be poured in earthen plates and garnished with silver foil on each dish.

Note: Phirni comes out better with soaked and finely ground rice paste. To give it extra creamy taste add half cup cream in boiling milk.

75

Rice Kheer

Milk — 1 kg
Rice — 75 gms
Sugar to taste — 100 gms (approx)
Chopped almonds, powdered green cardamom seeds,
Raisins etc. to garnish.

Wash and soak rice in little water. Boil milk. Add rice to
the milk and let it cook on a slow fire-keep stirring till rice is
well cooked and well assimilated with milk. Remove from
fire, add sugar, stir, let it cool. Add raisins and elaichi
powder. Put it in a bowl. Garnish with chopped almonds.
Serve cold. Can also be served hot. Goes well with poora.
Kheer-poora is welcome in 'Sawan'—the rainy season.

Note : Use Buffalo's milk—add ½ cup cream (malai) to
it when the milk boils

76

Phenian-di-Kheer

Fresh milk—1 kg
Phenian—2 large
Sugar to taste—100 gms (approx.)
Garnish with almonds
Flavour with green or brown elaichi powder.

Heat milk, add phenian and let it cook while stirring. It cooks fast and blends well. Add sugar and elaichi powder. Serve hot garnished with almonds-or chill and serve.

Note: 'Phenian' are specially made around '*Karva Chauth*'. Women take these with milk before starting the fast. It is a speciality from Amritsar.

Ghia-di-Kheer (Green Gourd Kheer)

Ghia (Green long gourd—400-500 gms)
tender without hard seeds
Whole milk—2 kg
Sugar to taste—200 gms
Cream (malai-top of milk)—1 cup
Garnish with raisins and powdered cardamom seeds
and blanched almonds

Scrape gourd and grate fine. Cook grated gourd in little water in pressure cooker for a few minutes. Boil milk, add boiled ghia Let it cook for ½ hour on slow fire till it is thick like rabri. Remove from fire, add sugar. Put it in a bowl and chill. Garnish with powdered cardamom, chopped almonds. Soak 50 gms raisins in water. Squeeze, add to the Kheer.

Rauh-di-Kheer (Sugarcane Juice Kheer)

Sugarcane juice—2 litres
Rice—200 gms
Grated carrots—250 gms
Milk—500 ml
Almonds—20
Raisins—20
Cardamom seeds—½ tsp
Fresh cream

Soak rice. Boil the juice-add ½ litre milk, simmer on slow fire. Keep on removing the scum till juice looks clean and clear-add rice, carrots and cardamom seeds, cook on slow fire till cooked. Add chopped almonds and raisins. Save some almonds to garnish.

Serve hot or cold with cream.

It is a popular winter sweet-dish specially made on 'Lohri'.

Gajar-di-Kheer (Carrot Kheer)

Milk—1 kg
Carrots—1|2 kg
Sugar to taste
Brown cardamom powdered—2
Almonds chopped—a few
Raisins (Saugi)—a few pieces

Wash, scrape and grate the carrots. Boil the milk-add grated carrots and let cook at medium fire till the carrots are cooked and milk has thickened. Add sugar and powdered cardamoms. Serve hot or cold garnished with chopped almonds and raisins. Serve with breakfast instead of wheat porridge (Dalia).

Maal Poora

Milk—*1 litre*
Flour—*1 level cup*
A pinch of soda-bi-carb   } *Sift together*
Sooji—*1 tbsp*
Milk—$\frac{1}{2}$ cup for flour
Sugar—$1\frac{1}{2}$ cup
Water—*1 cup*   } *for syrup*
Citric acid—$\frac{1}{2}$ tsp
Chopped pistachio—*10*
Chopped almonds—*10*
Kewra essence—$1\frac{1}{2}$ tbsp
Silver foil—(*Varq*)
Ghee or cooking oil for frying.

Put the milk on fire and stir till it is thick. Cool it. Mix flour, sooji and soda into this milk and make a smooth mixture. If the mixture is too thick-add $\frac{1}{2}$ cup of milk, little at a time. Make sticky syrup with sugar and water. Add citric acid when the syrup boils. Cool the syrup a little. Heat oil in the frying pan. Put the mixture with a round spoon and spread over the oil, turn it when slightly golden brown. Put it in the syrup and keep it soaked. Make more pooras and soak them-for sometime in the syrup. Remove from the syrup and put them in a serving dish. Decorate with silver foil, pistachio and almonds. Serve it with Kheer.

S'aada Poora (Plain Poora)

Sieved flour (maida)—8 tbsp
Sugar—4 tbsp
Saunf (aniseed)—1 tsp
Seeds of 2 brown cardamom
Water to make batter
Ghee or oil for frying

Sieve flour, add aniseed and cardamom seeds to it. Add sugar and make batter, add some water and stir to avoid lumps. Add enough water to make batter neither too thin nor thick. It should spread easily.

Heat 1 tbsp oil in frying pan. Spread two table poonfuls of batter. Fry it golden brown and turn do not let the oil smoke. Serve it hot with rice kheer.

Kheer-Poora is a delightful combination associated with the rainy day of Sawan.

81

Rabri

Milk—3 cups
Khoya—$\frac{1}{2}$ cup grated
Sugar—$\frac{3}{4}$ cup
Pistachio—10 (chopped)
Green cardamom—3 powdered
Silver foil (Varq)

Boil milk, add Khoya and Sugar. Simmer it till quantity is reduced to half. Into this add some chopped pistachios and powdered cardamom, put it in a dish garnish with rest of pistachio and put silver foil. Chill it and serve.

82

Kulfi

Milk—1 litre
Cream—100 gms
Sugar—50 gms or to taste
Cornflour—1 tbsp
Almonds—10
Green cardamom seed powdered—$\frac{1}{2}$ tsp
Kesar : a pinch
Kulfi moulds—6
Chopped pistachio—1 tbsp

Heat the milk, add cream or malai to it and let it boil till half of it is left. Stir cornflour in little cold milk and pour it in the thickened milk drop by drop while stirring the milk constantly. Cook for 2-3 minutes while stirring. Add sugar and cook. Remove from fire, let it cool, soak saffron in little water. Put the mixture in the liquidiser, add almonds and cardamom seeds and shake it up. Add saffron. Put the mixture, in kulfi moulds. Keep the freezer temperature on very cold and freeze the kulfis, takes 4-5 hours. Serve when fully set.

Falooda goes well with it.

83

Bhugga

[This preparation is made around 'Lohri' festival.
It is a winter delicacy and a great speciality.]

Khoya—1kg
White sesame seed (Til)—250 gms
to be cleaned thoroughly
Ground sugar—500 gms
Dry fruit : raisins, almonds, powdered
brown cardamom, grated dry coconut.

Heat khoya in a karahi—toss and turn—heat it well.
Coarsely pound the sesame seed. Remove khoya from fire,
add the til and sugar. Mix well. Add the dry fruit, chopped
almonds—powdered cardamom seeds—grated dry coconut.
Mix well. Let it cool a bit. Convert it into balls flatten
each—decorate with powdered cardamom seeds on top. Can
keep it for a few days.

Use boora cheeni for powdered sugar.

84

Pinni-Maanh-di-Dall-di

Urad dhuli (Black Gram split and washed—250 gms
Gram flour—125 gms
Pure ghee-- 250 gms to fry daal
Pure ghee—100 gms to fry gram flour
Chaar Goondan (gum blobs)—50 gms
Pistachio—15
Almonds—15
Raisins—15 to 20
Cashewnuts—10 to 15
Green cardomom (Powder the seeds)—10
Syrup sugar—350 gms
Water—1 cup

Soak Urad Daal for a few hours. Drain water and grind it
fine. Heat ghee in Karahi, fry daal in it. Keep turning and
tossing while it fries. Fry it brown. Take it out of the karahi.
Heat more ghee and fry katira goond light brown. Cool and
grind it to powder. In the same ghee fry gram flour brown,
stirring all the time. Chop pistachio, almonds and cashew
nuts. Powder cardamom seeds. Add all the dry fruit to the
fried daal, add fried gram flour and powdered katira goond.

Make thick syrup with sugar and water, make it two thread
consistancy. Add it to the fried ingredients and stir. Syrup
will get absorbed. Let it cool. Make Pinnis (ball sized) while
it is still warm. Pinnis stay for long.

Note. Katira Goond is collected off the kikar tree bark. It is a binder. And if soaked and taken with milk in summer, it is very cooling and refreshing. Chaar Goondan are available from the grocery shop. Addition of goondan give special taste and texture to pinnis.

85

Sooji-di-Pinni

Semolina (sooji)—1 kg
Khoya—500 gms
Ground sugar—600 gms
Pure ghee—350 gms
Dry fruit—grated coconut—chopped
almonds, magaz, raisins
Luke warm milk—1 cup
Some milk in a pan to moist the hands

Roast semolina in Karahi till it turns golden. Add ghee to semolina and on slow fire roast further till it leaves ghee. Crumble khoya and roast lightly in the karahi. Add it to roasted semolina. Add ground sugar and remove fire. Add dry fruit. Take 1 cup luke warm milk and add to the semolina-khoya mixture and blend it well with hands. Moist hands with milk and make medium sized balls. Put aside till dry. Can be kept for many days in air—tight container.

86

Jalebi (Sweet Mithai)

Maida—200 gms
Sour curd—30 gms
Warm water
Orange colour—a few drops
Oil for frying
Syrup
Sugar—225 gms
Water—115 gms

Take sour curd, sieve maida, make batter with curd, add little warm water to make it thick dropping consistency—add a few drops of orange colour. Put the batter aside for a few hours to ferment a little. Heat oil in a Karahi. Put the batter in a piping bag and in the oil make circles within circle. Make a few and fry them golden. Make thick syrup with sugar and water, dip jalebis in the syrup, take out and serve them hot.

Gulab Jamun

Khoya—250 gms
Maida—100 gms-sieve the flour
Beaten curds—½ cup
Soda-bi-carb—½ tsp
Oil or ghee for frying
Syrup
Water—2½ cups ⎫
           ⎬*boil together*
Sugar—12 tbsp ⎭
Keora essence

Mix soda in khoya and blend it well and mix sieved maida with it. Gradually add curds to it and knead well—Make 20 equal size balls.

Heat ghee—deep fry khoya balls, till light brown, the ghee should not get smoked. Fry on medium heat.

Syrup.   Heat water and sugar— boil for five minutes—clear the syrup by adding a little milk, add keora essence. Soak gulab jamuns in a pan in hot syrup. Garnish each Gulab Jamun with blanched almonds.

Shakkhar-Paar

Refined flour—3/4 cup
Wheat flour—1/4 cup
Vanaspti ghee—1 tbsp
Water to knead—1/3 cup
A small pinch of soda
Ghee or oil for frying

Syrup

Gur—250 gms
Water—½ cup
Small Pinch of Soda-bi-carb

Sieve flours together, add soda, rub in ghee and knead it well adding water. Take a ball of the dough roll out ½" inch thick, and cut into ½" wide and 2" long strips. Heat ghee in Karahi, fry the strips on medium fire till it is light brown. Pound gur, add water—put it on fire and cook to form soft ball consistency. Add fried strips to it and toss—each piece will get coated with gur, syrup, keep turning and tossing, syrup will dry.

Balu Shahi

Maida—2 cups
Ghee—½ cup
Curds—½ 2cup
Soda-bi-carb—1/4 tsp
Sugar--2 cups
Water—½ cup

Sift maida, add soda, rub in ghee, knead well with curds. Take medium sized doughball, flatten and make depression in the middle. Heat ghee in karahi, put the flattened balls in it—remove from fire—cook as long as the ghee simmers—put it back on low heat, fry till it is light brown. Make thick syrup with sugar and water: syrup should be one thread consistency. Dip fried balls in it. Remove after one minute, spread them in a plate (thali) to cool. Each ball gets coated with sugar. Sugar syrup should be of coating consistency.

Panjiri

Wheat flour—250 gms
Pure ghee—100 gms
Ground sugar—250 gms
Brown cardamom—2
Almond—10
Raisins—10 a few
Ginger powder—1/4 tsp
Grated dry coconut
Magaz seeds—1 tbsp

Heat ghee, fry flour, golden brown. Remove from fire, add ground sugar, add dry fruit, mix and store.

It is a nourisher and is given after childbirth. Ginger powder is good for inducing labour pains. This nutritious food is also good for keeping the expectant mother fit and healthy. It is generally given from the 5th—6th month of pregnancy. It has quite a tradition of acceptance behind it.

Besan-di-Barfi

Gram flour—2 cups
Pure ghee—3/4 cup
Milk—1/4 cup
Sugar—2 cups
Water—½ cup
Almonds—10
Powdered brown cardamom seeds—2 tsp

Mix 2 tbsp ghee with milk and gram flour. Heat rest of the ghee in a karahi, add gram flour, fry on medium fire stirring all the time, till it is golden brown. Make thick syrup with water and sugar. Add it to the fried gram flour. Stir and mix, and let extra water dry. Grease a plate or thali, pour it on that. Sprinkle powdered cardamom and chopped almonds on it. Let it set. Cut in diamonds when set. It stays for many days.

92

Akhrot-in-Gur

(Walnut Toffee)

Pounded gur—1 cup
Pure ghee—1 tbsp.
Walnuts— ½ cup
Tymol seeds—1/4 tsp
Milk—2 tsp

Heat ghee, add gur to it and stir, cook for a minute stirring, add tymol seeds and stir in walnuts. Remove from fire. Let it cool. Make balls of the prepared mixture and serve. Can be stored.

It is a winter delicacy.

Pickles, Chutneys, Preserves

No Punjabi meal is complete without varieties of pickles and chutneys made from seasonal fruit and vegetables. Fruit preserves are nourishing as well as medicinal.

93. Achar gobhi-shalgam-gajar
94. Mango pickle
95. Suhanjena-da-achar
96. Chillie pickle
97. Khatta-mitha amb-da-achar
98. Sabat nimbu-da-achar
99. Murge-da-achar
100. Chutneys and preserves:
    - Tamarind (imli) chutney
    - Pudina Chutney
    - Mango chutney
    - Tomato chutney
    - Chilly chutney
    - Gajar morabba
    - Amb-da-murabba

Achar Gobhi-Shalgam-Gajar (Pickle-Turnip) Cauliflower and Carrot-Sweet and Sour)

Vegetables : Turnips-Cauliflower and Carrots peeled and thickly chopped—8 kg in weight.

Gur—1 kg
Red chillies (Degi mirach)—250 gms
Salt—½ kg
Mustard powder—½ kg
Vinegar—1 bottle
Ginger—½ kg
Onions—½ kg
Garlic—8 pods
Mustard oil—2½ kg
Black pepper—50 gms ⎫
Cuminseed—50 gms ⎬ *Grind together*
Nutmeg—1 ⎪
Cloves—20 ⎭
Turmeric powder—150 gms
Dry plums—a few pieces (optional)

Heat oil—deep fry chopped vegetables lightly. Coarsely pound gur and soak it in vinegar. Grind onions garlic and ginger together and fry in the oil. Add fried vegetables, ground spices, salt, chillies, mustard powder. Heat vinegar, dissolve gur in it. Strain and add to the mixed vegetables and masalas etc. Soak plums in water, wash and strain, add to the pickle. Put it in the jar cover with muslin cloth—put it out in the sun for a few days and shake the jar everyday.

94

Mango Pickle

Raw mangoes—2 kg
Mustard oil—500 ml
Salt—125 gms
Red chillies—75 gms
Fenugreek seeds—50 gms
Aniseed—125 gms
Nigella (Kalunji)—75 gms
Turmeric powder—1 tbsp

Cut mangoes into medium sized pieces. Rub some salt on these pieces and keep them on a sieve or a basket with holes and keep it tilted for the water to run out of the salted mangoes. Spread them on a cloth in the sun to dry the pieces (2 hours are enough).

Take some oil—put all the dry ingredients—add the mango pieces also. Add some more oil to make it oily.

Put it in the jar. Tie muslin cloth. Keep it aside for three days, add more oil—to cover the mango pieces nicely. Put the cover and keep it in the sun for 3-4 days and shake the jar everyday.

Dehla

Put salt on dehla—let the water run out. Dry them in the sun. Add them to the mango pickle when it is fully ready.

Mango pickle masala is used for chilly pickle also. Slit long green chillies. Fill them with masala of mango pickle, put them back in the jar with more masala.

95

Suhanjena-da-Achar (Tender Drumstick Pickle)

Tender drumsticks—1 kg
Salt—50 gms
Mustard seeds (Rye)—50 gms
Red chillies—50 gms
Turmeric powder—50 gms
Mustard oil—250 ml

Clean and wipe drumsticks. Chop into small pieces. Wash and dry the mustard seed and grind to powder. Rub salt, mustard seed powder, red chillies and turmeric powder on drumsticks. Put them in a jar with little oil and keep in the sun for two days—shake the jar. Smoke the oil, cool it—add to the drumsticks—cover and shake daily.

Note : If there is masala from Amb-da-achar drumsticks can be added to that.

96

Chillie Pickle

Green chillies—200 gms
Garlic—3 pods
Ginger—200 gms
Cuminseeds—50 gms (roast and powder it)
Mustard oil—300ml
Vinegar—½ cup
Salt to taste—3 tsp

Grind ginger and garlic together and lightly brown the paste in hot oil—add powdered cuminseed and brown it further.

Slit green chillies and add to the oil. Cook for a few minutes—add vinegar, cook till the oil comes on top and vinegar is absorbed. Add salt at the end. Bottle when it is cold.

97

Khatta-Mitha Amb-da-Achar

Grated Raw mangoes—1 kg
Onion chopped—$\frac{3}{4}$ kg
Mustard oil—350 ml
Vinegar—$\frac{1}{4}$ bottle
Sugar—250 gms
Salt—125 gms
Red chillies—1 tbsp
Turmeric powder—1 tbsp
Pepper—1 tbsp
Cuminseed—1 tbsp
Cardamom—15 to 20
Aesfoedia (ground)—1 tsp
Ani seed(Saunf)—1 tbsp
Nigella (kalunji seed)—2 tbsp
Fenugreek seed (metha)—2 tbsp

Pound together cardomom seeds, pepper, fenugreek seeds and aniseed. Mix vinegar and sugar. Mix chopped onions and mangoes, add all the powdered spices, vinegar and sugar, salt, chillies and turmeric powder, add mustard oil and mix it well. Put in a clean jar. Tie muslin cloth on the jar and put in the sun for two hours for two days. Shake the jar. It is ready to be eaten. Spices can be adjusted to taste. This pickle does not stay for very long.

98

Sabat Nimbu-da-Achar

Lemons—1 kg
Salt— 200 gms
Black pepper—-25 gms
Mixed spices (Garam masala)—25 gms
Tymol seeds (Aijwain)—25 gms
Black salt—25 gms
Red chilli powder to taste
Sugar—½ kg

Soak the lemons in water for two days. Change the water daily. Take lemons out of water and wipe them dry. Keep aside 5 lemons. Make four Vertical cuts on each lemon. Put them in a jar and pour salt, pepper, mixed spices, tymol seeds and sugar and mix well. Squeeze the juice out of the lemons, kept aside. Add it to the lemons in the jar. Shake the jar well. Place the jar in the sun for two-three hours for two-three days. Pickle will be ready within a fortnight but with time will mature and taste better. It is important to shake the jar every day till the pickle is ready.

99

Murge-da-Achar (Chicken Pickle)

(Broiler) Chicken pieces—5 kg
Mustard oil—1 litre
Mustard (Rye)—325 gms
Cuminseed—100 gms
Brown cardamom—100 gms
Nutmeg—3
Degi mirach—½ packet
Salt to taste—about 5 tbsp
Turmeric—125 gms
Onions—½ kg
Ginger—200 gms
Garlic—200 gms
Vinegar—¾ bottle
Jar (maratban)

Smoke mustard oil in karahi. Clean and wipe chicken pieces and deep fry them light golden. If it is not a broiler then lightly pressure cook the chicken pieces in little water and then fry the chiken pieces.

Prepare the dry spices. Clean and powder mustard (rye). Grind cardamom seeds—cuminseed and nutmeg together.

Chop onion, grate the ginger, peel the garlic and grind together to a paste. In the same oil fry this masala brown. Add fried chicken and dry spices. Add vinegar and pack the pickle in the jar and put it out in the sun for a few days. Mustard takes a few days to assimilate. If the oil is not enough, more smoked oil may be added. Shake the jar daily.

100

Chutneys and Preserves

1. Tamarind Imli Chutney

Tamarind (Imli)—200 gms.
Jaggery (Shakkar)—100 gms.
Black salt—1 tbsp
White salt—1 tbsp
Roasted and ground cuminseed—1 tbsp
Red chilli powder—½ tbsp
Mint leaves—a few

Soak tamarind in water for 2 hours. Mash and strain. Add other ingredients and cook on fire stirring to get thick consistency. Add mint leaves.

2. Pudina Chutney

Fresh mint leaves—1 bunch
Onion—1
Ginger—Small piece
Garlic—2 cloves
Unripe mango peeled—1 small
or 1 tbsp pomegranate seeds
Green Chillies—2
Salt—1 tbsp
Sugar—2 tbsp

Grind the ingredients to a paste adding some water.

3. Mango Chutney

Grated raw mangoes—1 kg
Sugar—1 kg
Vinegar—½ bottle
Water for sugar syrup—¾ cup
Garlic—2 pods
Black pepper-salt-red chillies—to taste
Cloves—10
Cinnamon—2 sticks
Big cardamom (seeds)—15
Aniseed—1½ tbsp

Powder cloves, cinnamon cardamom seeds and aniseed together. Peel and grate the mangoes. Cook sugar and water to make one thread consistency syrup, then add the grated mangoes. Peel and grind the garlic. Add it to the mangoes with all the dry ingredients. Cook till it thickens. Remove from fire. Add vineger. Bottle immediately.

4. Tomato Chutney

Tomatoes—500 gms
Sugar—250 gms
Vinegar—160 ml

Mixed spices (Garam masala) -100 gms made from coriander seeds, cuminseed, cloves, pepper corns, cardamom blown, powder these. Salt and red chillies to taste.

Soak ripe tomatoes in hot water for five minutes, remove the skin and chop them in bits. Make paste with garam masala and a little vinegar. Put the rest of the vinegar in tomatoes and cook. After 15 minutes add sugar and garam masala paste, salt and chillies, cook till it thickens. Goes well with pranthas.

155

5. Chilli Chutney

Fresh coriander—3 bunches
Salt to taste
Chillies green—100 gms

Grind well to a fine paste or green chillies, salt and 2-3 cloves of garlic, ground together, make nice hot chutney. It goes well with plain Makki-di-Roti.

6. Carrot Preserve (Gajar Murabba)

Carrots—1 kg (small and tender)
Sugar—1 kg

Wash and scrape the carrots. Prick the carrots. Boil for 3-4 minutes in enough water to cover the carrots. Remove from fire. Add 1 kg sugar. Cover it and put it aside. Soak in sugar overnight.

Cook on very slow fire in the morning for 10-12 minutes. Put it aside. In the evening again cook for 5 minutes. Sugar should not be thread consistency. Next morning again cook for 5 minutes on very slow fire, and store.

7. Amb-da-Murabba

Mango slivers—1kg
Sugar—1 kg
Citric acid—$\frac{1}{2}$ tea spoon
Water—300 ml

Take good quality tight unripe mangoes. Wash them. Peel the mangoes and cut thick slivers. Keep them dipped in salted water to avoid them turning black.

Put these slivers in muslin cloth and lower the muslin bag in boiling water and keep it there for 5-10 minutes. Take out the bag open it prick the mango silvers with fork and keep aside for some time.

Make syrup with sugar and water and stir citric acid in it. Boil it to make thick syrup, keep it aside. Put mango slivers in it and cover the pan. Then again cook it till syrup is two thread consistency. Remove from fire.

Cool it and pack in clean jar and cover. Keep in a dry and cool place.

Spices in Punjabi Food

Food without spices is a sick man's food. Least of all Punjabis would eat bland food. Punjabi food is moderately spiced and flavoured with dry spices and fresh greens. For cooking a Punjabi meal, onion, garlic, ginger tomatoes are a must. Use of dry whole and powdered spices add to the flavour and taste. Chopped green coriander leaves garnish and enhance the flavour. Spices make the food aromatic and palatable.

1. Chaat Masala

Salt—2 tsp
Cuminseed—2 tsp
Dry ginger powder—1 tsp
Red chilli powder—1 tsp
Black pepper—½ tsp
Dry mango powder—4 tsp
Black salt—2 tsp

Grind and mix together.

2. Mixed Dry Spices-Powder (Garam Masala)

Cuminseed—50 gms
Cloves—10 gms

Cinnamon—10 gms.
Pepper corn.—20 gms.
Cardamom—50 gms.
Coriander seeds—50 gms.

Put all the spices in a thali and leave it in the sun for a few hours. Grind them together. Sieve through a fine sieve and store in a jar.

3. Gravy Masala

It is a base for many dishes. Onion-ginger, tomatoes are used liberally in Punjabi food. Curries are made with base of masala paste, garlic and ginger are ground to a paste and added to the ground onions or all the three are ground together. To make things easier electric blender is used to make masala paste. It takes time to fry it. Flavour, taste and the colour of the gravy depends mainly on the quality of fried masala. Tomatoes are added to give colour taste and thickness. Curdase substituted for tomatoes. Onions-garlic giner tomotoes all are chopped and with little water can be pressure cooked for five minutes and then after drying the water, mashed and fried in cooking oil with dry spcies etc. It is a simpler and faster way of doing the masala. Fried masala can be stored in the freezer.

4. Turka

It is a commonly used term in Punjabi cooking. Turka is the final stage of a dish. It is to enhance the taste. Dal or saag is bland without Turka. Butter or pure ghee is invariably used for Turkas. For making some vegetables without gravy-turka of cumminseed or onions and ginger is first made and then other ingredients added.

5. Punjabi Masala Tea (Spiced Tea)

Grind together
Aniseed—3/4 tsp
Brown cardamom—4
Cinnamon stick—1
Cloves—4
Water-milk-sugar
Tea leaves—1 tsp

Add ½ tsp masala to 1 cup water and boil for two minutes, add milk and sugar to taste, add tea leaves bring to a boil, lower the heat-let the tea brew for a minute. Strain and serve it hot.

Glossary

Condiments

Almond	Badam
Aniseed	Heeng
Asafeotida	Saunf
Basil	Tej patta
Bay leaf	Tulsi
Black salt	Kala namak
Cardamom	Elaichi (Green or brown)
Cinnamon	Dalchini
Cloves	Laung
Cuminseed (black or white)	Jeera
Coriander leaves	Hara dhania
Coriander seeds	Sookha dhania
Coconut	Narial, dry or fresh
Curri leaves	Meethi-neem-ke-patte karhi patta
Dhingri	a kind of mushroom patta
Fenugreek	Methi
Gur	Sugarcane juice boiled and set
Ginger (dry)	Sonth-sundh
Guchhi	a kind of mushroom
Jaggery	Unrefined brown sugar (Shakkar)
Mace	Jaiviteri
Mustard seed	Rye

Onion Seed Nigella	Kalaunji
Mango powder	Amchoor
Magaz	Dried peeled seeds of pumpkin cucumber marrow and water melon
Nutmeg	Jaipal
Pepper corns	Kali mirach
Poppy seeds	Khas-Khas
Pomegranate seeds	Anardana
Pistachio	Pista
Raisin	Saugi
Refined flour	Maida
Turmeric	Haldi
Tamarind	Imli
Saffron	Kesar
Silver foil	Varq
Semolina	Sooji
Vinegar	Sirka
Whey	Panir-da-pani
Degi mirach	Kashmiri mirach, known for its colour and flavour
Kateera goond	Gum taken off keekar tree bark. It is used as a binder.
Chaar goondan	edible gums

Vegetables (Sabzi)

Fenugreek	Methi
Spinach	Palak
Mustard greens	Sarson-da-saag
Coriander	Dhania
Mint	Pudina
Cabbage	Bund gobi
Colocasia	Arbi
Lotus root	Bhein-kamal kakkri

Radish	Mooli
Turnip	Shalgam
Yam	Zimikand
Bathoo	A kind of green
Brinjal	Baingan
Bitter gourd	Karela
Green gourd	Lauki
Elephand yam	Zimikand
Cucumber	Khira
Pumpkin	Halwa kaddu
Wate melon	Tarbuz
Carrot	Gajar
Peas	Mattar
Tomato	Tamatar
Potato	Alu
Onion	Piaz
Garlic	Lassan
Ginger	Adrak
Lady finger	Bhindi
Capsicum	Shimla mirach
Green chillies	Hari mirach
Red chillies	Lal mirach
Jack fruit	Kathal
Lettuce	Salad patta
Mushroom	Khumb
Ridge gourd	Hari torai
French beans	Fras beans

Pulses and Cereals

Whole green gram	Mung sabat
Red gram	Arhar
Bengal gram	Channa daal (chholian-di-dall)
Bengal gram whole	Kale channe

Green gram washed	Dhulli mung
White gram	Kabli channa-chittee chhole
Gram flour	Vesan
Whole black lentil	Masur sabat.
Split lentil	Masoor dhuli
Black gram	Maanh sabat (Kali daal, urad saabat)
Kidney beans	Rajmanh
Black gram split and washed	Urad dhuli-washed
Refined flour	Maida.

Utensils and Kitchen Equipment in Punjabi Kitchen

In olden days there was exquisite aroma emnating from the food cooked in Karahi (earthen pot) on chulhas and angithis with hot tandoori-rotis baked in earthen tandoor. Even now in villages food is cooked in the same old fashion. Cooking done in earthen-pots gives a distinct flavour and cooks better on slow fire, tastes delicious and is more nutritious. Gas and pressure cookers have brought revolution in cooking methods at the cost of taste and aroma. Dal and saag cooked in degkchi or karahi on slow fire have distinct taste and flavour. Butter-milk churned in earthen pot has its own taste. Old devices produce better and original taste and result.

Utensils

Degkchi or Patila	Saucepan
Pittal-ki-karahi	Brass deep frying pan
Tawa (thick or thin)	Griddle
Karchi	For stirring, long handled ladle, metal stirrer
Chakla	Round board—for rotis etc.
Belana	Rolling pin

Mathni or Madhani	Wooden churner
Dauri	Pestle
Darda	Mortar for grinding masalas etc.
Chaku	Knife
Thali	Round metal plate with high edges.
Kunda	Earthen pot for setting curds
Ghara	Earthen pot liquid (container)
Lohe-di-karahi	Iron Pan
Maratban	Glass or ceramic jar
Chhanini	Strainer for flour etc.
Poni	Strainer for deep frying
Madhana	Wooden masher
Karhni	Earthen cooking pot
Khonchi	Flat ladel
Kauli	Katori made of steel or brass
Wooden spoon	for mixing and lifting out pickles
Daatri	For chopping saag
Chatti	Earthen pot for churning buttermilk (lassi)
Hamam-dasta	Iron vessel and bar for pounding and grinding dry spices.